WOODSCRAFT NATION

D. W. POWELL

ROBIN L. POWELL

MOtivational PRESS®

LEADERS IN GLOBAL PUBLISHING

Published by Motivational Press, Inc.
1777 Aurora Road
Melbourne, Florida, 32935
www.MotivationalPress.com

Manufactured in the United States of America.

ISBN: 978-1-62865-426-4

CONTENTS

PREFACE

F OR MOST OF MY SIXTY some years I have studied, learned, lived and enjoyed the out of doors. As a child, I ran free in the pine woods and the marsh peat bog swamps in Largo, Florida. Growing up I found the Native American way of life and religion fit my understanding of how the world worked and where I would fit into it. The woods, fields, marshes, and swamps became not only where I learned and grew, but where the self-discovery of nature, and self-reliance took place.

This book is a rewrite of sorts dedicated to the knowledge within and without normal academia. "Woodscraft" is namely the development or revival as a school of thought for women and men as was written in the original "Woodcraft" by Ernest Thompson Seton in the early 1900s. It is a bit of a paradigm shift from our traditional way of learning.

"Woodscraft" is a guide for outdoor life with the adventure of all the sciences included. As the model for outdoor life in the U.S.A., we look first at the ways of Native Americans. In the sections called Spartans of the West and Campfire Stories of Indian Character, you will find a new way of thinking and understanding of those who endured and came before us.

My dream of sharing this book of skills and life lessons will move this generation and the next to personal accountability and personal leadership in all they do.

Our initial plan was to update the original Woodcraft book, alter requirements for the twenty-first century, and add resources readily available today like the internet. As we worked through the 600-page original book, we altered this so Woodscraft became less wordy and detailed hoping more readers will feel inspired to fulfill the requirements on their own. We hope readers become aware of their surroundings and more in tune with the natural world.

The result is this "Woodscraft Nation" book – a combination of the original "Woodcraft" by Seton and our experiences and expectations through working with youth and adults in the outdoor arena.

We hope everyone – all cultures, genders, and ages – find the "requirements" attainable and realistic throughout the book.

WOODSCRAFT NATION

FOUNDATION

THIS IS A TIME WHEN THE whole nation is turning toward
the principles of Outdoor Living, seeking the physical
regeneration so needed for continued national existence. We are
waking to the fact long known to thoughtful women and men, that
those who live longest live nearest to the ground – that is, those
who live a simple life of primitive times live longer and healthier.

Depression has plagued man since moving from caves into
houses. People need the sun and fresh air and all that they offer.
It can heal many of the ills of the mind, body, and spirit. Go
outside and play – no matter how old you are or how bad you
are feeling.

Sports are the great incentive to Outdoor Life. Nature Study
is the intellectual side of sports. Spend time outside playing and
experiencing nature.

I should like to lead this whole nation into the way of living outdoors for at least a month a year, reviving and expanding a custom that as far back as Moses was deemed essential to the national well-being.

Not long ago a benevolent rich man, impressed with this idea, chartered a bus and took some hundreds of city boys up into the mountains for a day in the woods. The boys were excited to get out of the city! When they got off the bus, they were told to go explore, and make sure to use the "buddy system" where at least two stay together and watch out for each other. The boys disappeared quickly and turned to what they knew. Checking their cell phones for a connection, playing games on their phones, smoking, playing cards, and just standing around, looking lost and bored.

The well-meaning wealthy man learned quickly that it is not enough to take the boys outdoors. He would have to teach them how to enjoy and survive in it.

When two or three young people camp out, they can live as a sort of family, especially if a grown-up will be with them; but when a dozen or more are of the party, it is necessary to organize. What manner of organization will be practical, and also give full recognition to the nine principles of Woodscraft?

1. Recreation
2. Outdoor Living
3. Self-rule
4. The Campfire
5. Woodscraft Traditions
6. Honors by Standards

7. Personal decoration for personal achievement

8. A Heroic Ideal

9. Picturesqueness in all things

The Tribal or Native American form of organization works the best in most of these situations. Fundamentally, this is a republic or limited monarchy, and many experiments have proved it best for our purpose. It makes members self-governing. It offers appropriate things to do outdoors. It is so flexible that it can be adopted in whole or in part, at once or gradually. Its picturesqueness takes immediate hold and it lends itself well to our objective.

A large band of people have never camped out or been together for a week or a month without finding it necessary to recognize a *leader* or ruling set whose position rests on merit, some wise, grown person to guide them in difficulties, and a place to display *the emblems* of the camp. That is, they have adopted the system of Chief, Council, Medicine Man/Women and Totem Pole.

The ideal Native American stands for the highest type of primitive life. They were masters of Woodcraft, morally sound, clean, womanly, manly, heroic, reverent, truthful, self-controlled, and picturesque, always.

America owes much to the Native American. When the struggle for freedom came, it was between men of the same blood and bone, equal in brains and in strength. The British had better equipment. The great advantage of the American Patriot was that he was trained in the ways of the Native tribes. This lead to victory.

The Native American can do no greater service now and in the future. He can teach us the ways of outdoor life, the nobility of courage, the joy of beauty, the blessedness of "enough", the glory of service, the power of kindness, and peace of mind. For these were the things that the Native American stood for. These are the sum of his faith.

Nine leading principles to keep in mind:

RECREATION

This movement is for *recreation and re-creation.*

OUTDOOR LIVING

Camping is the simple life reduced to actual practice, as well as the culmination of the outdoor life. Camping has no great popularity today because women and men have the idea that it is an expensive journey to the wilderness. Some think that it is inconvenient, dirty, and dangerous. These are misconceptions that have arisen because camping as an art is not understood. When intelligently followed, camp-life must take its place as a less expensive and delightful way of living, as well as a mental and physical savior of those strained or broken by the grind of the over-busy world.

The wilderness affords the ideal camping opportunity, but many of the benefits can be attained by living in a tent on a town lot, the backyard, a piazza, or even a housetop.

SELF-GOVERNMENT WITH ADULT GUIDANCE.

Control from without is a poor thing when you can get control from within. As far as possible, then, we make these camps self-governing. Each full member has a vote in affairs.

THE MAGIC OF THE CAMPFIRE.

What is a camp without a campfire? – not a camp at all, but a chilly place in a landscape, where some people happen to have some things. When first the brutal anthropoid (early human) stood up and walked erect, the great event was symbolized and marked by the lighting of the very first campfire.

For millions of years our race has seen in this blessed fire, the means and emblem of light, warmth, protection, councils, and friendly gatherings. The spell cannot be found in the electric heater, flickering logs on the monitor, or even the gas logs in the fire place that will reach the heart in the same way as a campfire. Only the ancient sacred fire of burning wood has the power to touch and thrill the chords of primitive remembrance.

When women and men sit together at the campfire they seem to shed all modern form and poise, and look back to the primitive. Having camped in peace together, forms a lasting bond of union – however wide your worlds may be apart. The campfire, then is the focal center of all primitive brotherhood.

WOODSCRAFT TRADITIONS.

Realizing that *womanhood and manhood, not scholarship,* is the first aim in education, we have sought out those pursuits which develop the finest character, the finest physique, and which may be followed out of doors, which, in a word, *make for womanhood and manhood.* Woodscraft is the accomplishment of an all-around Woods person – riding, hunting, camp-craft, tracking, mountaineering, Indian-craft, first aid, astronomy, signaling, and boating. To this we add all good outdoor athletics and sports, including sailing, nature study, and wild animal photography.

HONORS BY STANDARDS.

We have lost our competitive edge by the over use of rewards with no accomplishments. We see it rampant in our colleges today where every effort is made to discover and develop a champion while a great body of students is neglected. That is, the ones in need of physical development do not get it, and those who do not need it are over-developed. In our non-competitive tests the enemies are not *"the other fellows,"* but *time and space,* the forces of nature. We try *not to put down the others, but to raise ourselves.* Prizes are not honors.

PERSONAL DECORATION FOR PERSONAL ACHIEVEMENTS.

The love of glory is the strongest motive in a savage. Civilized man is supposed to master this impulse with high principles, values and morals. But those who believe that the women, men, girls and boys, are civilized in this highest sense, would be greatly surprised if confronted with statistics. Nevertheless, a human weakness may be good material to work with in this endeavor of achievements. We need to face the facts as they stand. Each has a choice in personal decorations that all can see, have, and desire.

A HEROIC IDEAL.

The girl or boy from ten to fifteen, like the savage, is purely physical in their ideals. I do not know a girl or boy who would not like to be an Olympic athlete or a famous author. Therefore, I accept the fact, and seek to keep in view an ideal that is physical, but also clean, womanly, manly, heroic, already familiar, and leading with certainty to higher things.

PICTURESQUENESS IN EVERYTHING.

Very great importance should be attached to this. The effect of the picturesque is magical, and all the more subtle and irresistible because it is not on the face of it reasonable. The charm of titles and bright costumes, of the beautiful ceremony, phrase, dance, and song, are utilized in all ways. Picturesqueness is more about being well-balances, self-assured and confident.

THE SPARTIANS OF THE WEST, OUR NATIVE AMERICANS

N O WORLD MOVEMENT ever grew as a mere doctrine. It must have some noble example, a living, appealing personality, a woman/man to whom we can point to and say, "This is what we mean". All great faiths of the world have had such a woman/man, and for the lack of one, many great flawless truths have been long-forgotten.

To exemplify an outdoor movement, we felt we needed a man/woman who was of the Americas, who was physically fit, clean, pure, high-minded, heroic, picturesque, and a master of Woodscraft. We looked with in our own culture and race and found none that inspired or captured us. We looked back at King Arthur, Leif Ericsson, and Robin Hood, none met our requirements. There was but one figure that stood out to all the requirements and that was the Ideal Indian of James Fennimore Cooper's *Longfellow*.

For that reason, we chose the Native American, and called this organization Woodscraft". I have been told that using the

Native American will hurt this Woodscraft movement. If that so, it is because we do not know what the Native American was, and we shall make it part of our task to remove the prejudice.

We know more about the Native American today than we ever did. Indeed, we knew almost nothing of him in past years. We were given two pictures: one, the ideal savage of *Longfellow*, the primitive man, so noble in nature that he was incapable of anything small or mean or wicked and the other presented by those who coveted his possessions, and to justify their robberies, they sketched the Native American as a dirty, filthy, squalid wretch; a demon of cruelty and cowardice, incapable of human emotion, and never good 'til dead.

Which of these is the true picture? Let us calmly examine the pages of history, taking the words and records of the Native Americans and settlers, friends and foes of the Native American, and be prepared to render a verdict, in absolute accordance with that evidence, no matter where it leads us.

Let us begin by admitting that it is fair to take the best examples of the Native American, to represent their philosophy and goodness even as we ourselves would prefer being represented by John C. Maxwell, Stephen R. Covey, Jim Rohn and similar philosophers rather than by the border ruffians and cut-throat outlaws who were principle examples of our ways among the Native Americans.

It is freely admitted that in all tribes, at all times, there were reprobates and scoundrels, a reproach to the people just as amongst ourselves we have outcasts and criminals. But these were despised by their own people, and barely tolerated. Much like our own outcasts and criminals.

We must in fairness judge the Native American and his way of life and thought by exemplifications of his best types: Hiawatha, Wabasha I, Tshut-che-nau, Ma-to-to-pa, Tecumseh, Kanakuk, Chief Joseph, Dull Knife, Washakie, and many other people who were in no way touched by the doctrines of the settlers.

AMERICA FOR THE AMERICANS — TECUMSEH

O F ALL THE FIGURES in the light of Native American history, that of Tecumseh, or Tecumtha the "Leaping Panther," the war chief of the Shawnees, stands out perhaps highest and best as the ideal, noble, Native America.

His father was chief of the tribe. Tecumseh was born in 1768 at the village of the Piqua, near the site of Springfield, Ohio. Of all the natives, the Shawnees had been most energetic and farseeing in their opposition to the encroachments of the settlers. But the flood of invasion was too strong for them. The old chief fell, battling for home and people, at Point Pleasant in 1774. His eldest son followed his father's footsteps, and the second met death in a hopeless fight with Wayne in 1794, leaving young Tecumseh war chief of his tribe. At once he became a national figure. He devoted his whole life and strength to the task of saving his people from the settlers, and to that end resolved that he must first effect a national federation of all the tribes. Too often tribes had been pitted against tribe for the settler's advantage. In union alone he saw the way of salvation and to this end he set about an active campaign among the tribes of the Mississippi Valley.

His was no mean spirit of revenge; his mind was too noble for that. He hated the settlers as the destroyers of his race, but prisoners and the defenseless knew well that they could rely on his honor and humanity and were safe under his protection. When only a boy - for his military career began in childhood - he had witnessed the burning of a prisoner and the spectacle was so abhorrent to his feelings that by earnest and eloquent harangue he induced the party to give up the practice forever.

In later years, his name was accepted by helpless women and children as a guarantee of protection even in the midst of hostile natives. He was of commanding figure, nearly six feet in height and compactly built; of dignified bearing and piercing eye, before who's lightning even a British general quailed. His was the fiery eloquence of speech and the clear-cut logic of a masterful thinker. Abstemious in habit, charitable in thought and action, he was as brave as a lion, but humane and generous with all - in a word, a Native American Knight-errant, whose life was given to his people.

THE TEACHINGS OF WABASHA

IN THE DAY OF HIS strength no man is fat. Fat is good in a beast, but not in a man; it is disease and comes only of an evil life.

No man will eat three times each sun if he would keep his body strong and his mind unclouded.

Bathe every sun in cold water and one sun in seven enter the sweat lodge.

If you would purify your heart and so see clearer the way of the Great Spirit, touch no food for two days or more, according to your strength. For thereby your spirit have mastery over the body and the body is purged.

Touch not the poisonous firewater that makes wise men turn fools. Neither touch food nor taste drink that robs the body of its power or the spirit.

Guard your tongue in youth, and in age you may mature a thought that will be of service to your people.

Praise the Great Spirit when you rise, when you bathe, when you eat, when you meet friends and for all good happenings. And if so be you see no cause for praise the fault is in yourself.

A proven Minisino is at all time clean, courteous and master of himself.

The wise man will not hurt his mind for the passing pleasure of the body.

If any man is given over to sex appetite he is harboring a rattlesnake, whose sting is rottenness and sure death.

By prayer and fasting and fixed purpose you can rule your own spirit, and so have power over all those about you.

When your time comes to die, sing your death song and die pleasantly, not like the settler men whose hearts are filled with fear of death, so when the time comes, they weep and wail and pray for a little more time so they may live lives over again in a different manner.

THE NATIVE AMERICAN CREED

These are a compilation of the main thoughts and ideals in Native American Creeds:

While he believed in many gods, he accepted the idea of one Supreme Spirit, who was everywhere all the time, whose help was needed continually, and might be secured by prayer and sacrifice.

He believed in the immorality of the soul, and that its future condition was to be determined by its behavior in his present life.

He reverenced his body as the sacred temple of his spirit; and believed it is his duty in all ways to perfect his body that his earthly record might be the better. We cannot, short of ancient Greece, find his equal in physical perfection.

He believed in subjection of the body by fasting, whenever it seemed necessary for the absolute domination of the spirit; as when, in some great crisis, that spirit felt the need for better insight.

He believed in reverence for his parents, and in old age supported them, even as he expected his children to support him.

He believed in the sacredness of property. Theft among the Native Americans was unknown.

He believed that the murderer must expiate his crime with his life and that the nearest kin was the proper avenger, but that for accidental manslaughter compensation might be made in goods.

He believed in cleanliness of body.

He believed in purity of morals.

He believed in speaking the truth, and nothing but the truth. His promise was absolutely binding. He hated and despised a liar, and held all falsehood to be an abomination.

He believed in beautifying all things in his life. He had a song for every occasion – a beautiful prayer for every stress. His garments were made with painted patterns, feathers, and quill work. He had dances for every fireside. He has led the world in the making of beautiful baskets, blankets, and canoes. While the decorations he put on his lodges, weapons, clothes, dishes, dwellings, beds, cradles, or grave-boards were among the countless evidences of his pleasure in the beautiful, as he understood it.

He believed in the simple life. He held, first, that the land belonged to the tribe, not to the individual. Next, that the accumulation of property was the beginning of greed that grew into monstrous crime.

He believed in peace and the sacred obligations of hospitality.

He believed that the noblest of virtues was courage, and prayed for that above all other qualities. He believed that the most shameful of crimes was being afraid.

He believed that he should so live his life that fear of death could never enter his heart; that when the last call came he should put on the paint and honors of a hero going home, then sing his death song and meet the end in triumph.

If we measure this great pagan creed by the Ten Commandments, we shall find he accepted and obeyed them, all but the first and third, that is, he had many lesser gods beside the one Great Spirit, and he knew not the Sabbath Day of rest. His religious faith, therefore, was much the same as that of the mighty Greeks, before whom all the world of learning bows, not unlike that of many Christians.

THE MYTHS

These are the chief charges against the Native American:

First: *The Native American tribes were cruel to their enemies, even torturing them at the stake in extreme cases. He knew nothing about forgiving and loving them.*

In the main, this is true. But how much less cruel he was than the leaders of the Christian Church in the Middle Ages? What Native American massacre will compare with horrors of the Spanish Inquisition? There was no torture used by the Native Americans that was not also used by the Spaniards. Every frontiersman of the early days knows that in every outbreak the settlers were the aggressors and in every evil count – robbery, torture and massacre – they did exactly as the Native American's did. "The ferocity of the Native American," says Bourke, "has been more than equaled by the ferocity of the Christian."

There are good grounds that the Native Americans were cruel to their enemies, but it is surprising to see how little of this cruelty there was in primitive days. In most cases, the enemy was killed in battle or adopted into the tribe, very rarely was he tortured. Captain Clark says of the Cheyenne Tribe.

The settlers, however, had printed media (newspapers) to state their case, while the Native Americans had none to tell their story or defend themselves. Furthermore, it is notorious that all massacres of Native Americans by the settlers were accomplished by treachery *in times of peace*, while the Native American massacres of settlers were *in times of war*, to resist invasion.

Above all, Tecumseh was the ideal noble Native American who realized he was not alone. Wabasha, Osceola, Kanakuk, and Wovoka must be numbered among those whose great hearts reached out in kindness even to those who hated them. Tecumseh taught. "Love your enemy after he is conquered". Kanakuk preached non-resistance to evil. Wovoka, "Be *kind* to all men."

Second: *The Native American had no property instincts.*

He was a Socialist in all matters of large property, such as land, its fruits, rivers, fish, and game. So were the early Christians. All that believed were together; had all things in common, and sold their possessions and goods, and parted them to all men, as every man had need. They considered that every child had a right to a bringing up, and every old person to a free living from the tribe. We know that it worked well, for there was neither hunger nor poverty, except when the whole tribe was in want. We know also that there were among them no men of shameful, monstrous wealth.

Third: *He was not well prepared.*

All the old travelers testify that each village had its fields of corn, beans, and pumpkins. The crops were harvested and safely carried them over long periods when there was no other supply. They did not believe in vast accumulations of wealth, because their wise men had said greed would turn their hearts to stone and make them forget the poor. Furthermore, since all, when strong, contributed to the tribe, the tribe supported them in childhood, sickness and age. They had no poor. They had no famine until the traders came with whiskey and committed the *crimes for which as a nation have yet to answer.*

Fourth: *He was dirty.*

Many dirty habits are to be seen today among the Reservation Native Americans, but it was not so in the free days. A part of the old Native Americans religion was to take a bath every day the year round for the helping of his body. Some tribes twice a day. Every village had a sweat lodge (like a Turkish bath) in continual use. It is only the degraded Native American who has become dirty, and many of the settlers who often assail him as filthy never take a bath from birth to judgement day.

Fifth: *He was lazy.*

No one who saw the Native American in his ancient form agrees with this charge. He was not fond of commercial manufacturing, but the regular work of tilling his little patch of corn and beans he did not shirk, nor the labor of making weapons and boats, not the frightful toil of portaging, hunting and making war. Many men will not allow their horses to bare such burdens as the Chipewyan's bare daily, without a thought of hardship, accepting all as a part of their daily lot.

Sixth: *He degraded women to be a mere beast of burden.*

Some have said so, but the vast bulk of evidence today goes to show that while the women did the household drudgery and lighter tasks, the men did the work beyond their partner's strength. In making clothes, canoes, and weapons, as well as in tilling of the fields, men and women worked together. The women had a voice in all the great affairs, and a far better legal position than in most of the civilized world today.

Seventh: *He was treacherous.*

Primitive Native Americans never broke a treaty; his word was as good as his bond. The American Government broke every treaty as soon as there was something to gain by doing so. It would be easy to fill a large volume with startling and trustworthy testimony as to the goodness of the old Native American of the best type.

REVERENCE

In 1832 George Catlin, the painter, went West and spent eight years with the unchanged Native Americans of the Great Plains. He lived with them and became conversant with their lives. He has left one of the fullest and best records we have of the real Native American. Concerning the Native American's religion, he and others say:

"The North American Indian is everywhere, in his native state, a highly moral and religious being, endowed by his Maker with an intuitive knowledge of some great Author of his being, and the Universe, in dread of whose displeasure he constantly lives, with the apprehension before him a future state, where he expects to be rewarded or punished according to the merits he has gained or forfeited in his world.

"Morality and virtue, I venture to say the civilized world need not undertake to teach them.

"I never saw any other people of any color who spend so much of their lives in humbling themselves before and worshipping the Great Spirit." (Catlin)

"We have been told of late years that there is no evidence that any tribe ever believed in one overruling power; yet, in the early part of the seventeenth century, Jesuits and Puritans alike testified that tribes which they had met, believed in a god, and it is certain that, at the present time, many tribes worship a Supreme Being who is ruler of the Universe." (Grinnell)

A typical prayer is recorded for us by Grinnell.

"My Father (who dwells) in all places, it is through you that I am living. Perhaps it was through you that this man put me in this condition. You are the Ruler. Nothing is impossible with you. If you

see fit, take this (trouble) away from me. Now you, all fish of the rivers, and you all birds, and all animals that move upon the earth, and you, O Sun! I present to you this animal. You, birds in the air, and you, animals upon the earth, we are related; we are alike in this respect, that one Ruler made us all. You see how unhappy I am. If you have any power, intercede for me."

"In the life of the Native American there was only one inevitable duty, the duty of prayer – the daily recognition of the Unseen and Eternal. His daily devotions were more necessary to him than daily food. He wakes at daybreak, puts on his moccasins and steps down to the water's edge. Here he throws handfuls of clear cold water into his face, or plunges in boldly. After the bath, he stands erect before the advancing dawn, facing the sun as it dances upon the horizon, and offers his unspoken orison. His mate may proceed or follow him in his devotions, but never accompanies him. Each soul must meet the morning sun, the new, sweet earth, and the Great Silence alone!

In the light of all this evidence, is it to be wondered that most of the early historians who lived with the primitive Americans of the Plains, were led to believe, from their worship of God, their strict moral code, their rigid laws as to foods, clean and unclean, and their elaborate system of bathing and purification, that in these Native American peoples of the New World, they had indeed found the long-lost tribes of Israel?

CLEANLINESS

Catlin, after eight years in their lodges (1832-40), says that notwithstanding many exceptions, among the wild Natives the *"strictest regard to decency and cleanliness and elegance of dress is*

*observed, and there are few people, perhaps, who take more pains
to keep their persons neat and cleanly, than they do."*

*"In their bathing and ablutions at all seasons of the year, as
a part of their religious observances – having separate places for
men and women to perform these immersions."*

Every village in the old days had a Turkish bath, as we call
it, a "Sweat Lodge," as they say, used as a cure for inflammatory
rheumatism, etc. Catlin describes this in great detail and says:

*The "Sweat Lodge" is usually a low lodge covered with blankets
or skins. The patient goes in undressed and sits by a bucket of water.
In a fire outside, a number of stones are heated by the attendants.
These are rolled in, one or more at a time. The patient pours
water on them. This raises a cloud of steam. The lodge becomes
very hot. The individual drinks copious draughts of water. After
a sufficient sweat, he raises the cover and rushes into the water,
beside which the lodge is always built. After this he is rubbed down
with buckskin, and wrapped in a robe to cool off.*

This was used as a bath, as well a religious purification. I have
seen scores of them. Clark says they were "common to all tribes".
Every old-timer knows that they were in daily use by the Tribes
and scoffed at by the settlers who, indeed, were little given to
bathing of any kind.

CHASTITY

The Flatheads on the Buffalo Plains, generally encounter the
Pagans and fight desperately when attacked. They never attempt
war themselves, and have the character of a brave and virtuous
people, not in the least addicted to those vices so common among
savages who have had long interaction with Europeans. Chastity

is particularly esteemed, and no woman will barter her favors, even with settlers, upon any mercenary consideration. She may be easily prevailed upon to reside with a settler as his wife, according to the custom of the country, but prostitution is out of the question – she will listen to no proposals of that nature. The morals have not yet been sufficiently debauched and corrupted by an interaction with people who call themselves Christians, but whose licentious and lecherous manners are far worse than those of savages.

A striking example is to be seen throughout the Northwest country, of the depravity and wretchedness of the Natives, but as one advances into the interior parts, vice and debauchery become less frequent.

Happy are those who have the least connection with us, for most of the present depravity is easily traced to its origin in their interaction with settlers. That baneful source of all evils, spirituous liquor, has not yet been introduced among the Natives of the Columbia. To the introduction of that subtle poison among the savage tribes may be mainly attributed their miserable and wretched condition. (Henry)

Jonathan Carver, who traveled among the Sioux from 1766-9, says:

"Adultery is esteemed by them a heinous crime, and punished with great rigor."

BRAVERY

Old-time travelers and modern Native fighters agree that there was no braver man on earth, alive or in history, then the Native American warrior. Courage was the virtue he chiefly honored. His whole life and training were the purpose of making him calm, fearless and efficient in every possible stress or situation.

Father Lafitau said of the Eastern Tribes, in 1724 wrote,

"They are high-minded and proud; possess a courage equal to every trial; an intrepid valor; the most heroic constancy under torments, and an equanimity which neither misfortune nor reverses can shake."

"A Native meets death, when it approaches him in his hut, with the same resolution he has often faced in the field. His indifference relative to this important article, which is the source of so many apprehensions to almost every other nation, is truly admirable. When his fate is pronounced by the physician, and it remains no longer uncertain, he harangues those about him with the greatest composure." (Carver)

"The greatest insult that can be offered to any Native, is, to doubt his courage." (Hunter)

THRIFT AND PROVIDENCE

Every village in the old days had its granaries of corn, its stores of dried beans, berries, and pumpkin-strips, as well as its dried buffalo tongues, pemmican, and deer's meat. To this day, all the Fisher Tribes of the North and West dry great quantities of fish, as well as berries, for the famine months that are surely coming.

Many of the modern Tribes, armed with rifles, have learned to emulate the settlers, and slaughter game for the love of slaughter, without reference to the future. Such waste was condemned by the old-timers, as an abuse of the gifts of God, and which would surely bring its punishment.

"After all, the Wild Tribes could not justify termed improvident, when the manner of life is taken into consideration. They let nothing go to waste, and labored incessantly during the summer and fall to lay up provisions for the inclement season. Berries of all kinds were industriously gathered and dried in the sun. Even the wild cherries were pounded up, stones and all, made into cakes, and dried, for use in soups, and for mixing with the pounded jerked meat and fat to form a much-prized Native delicacy." (Eastman)

"The Tribes, except those who live adjoining to the European colonies, can form to themselves no idea of the value of money. They consider it, when they are made acquainted with the uses to which it is applied by other nations, as a source of innumerable evils. To it they attribute all the mischiefs that are prevalent among Europeans, such as treachery, plundering, devastations and murder." (Carver)

Could we have a more exact paraphrase of "The love of money is the root of all evil?"

Beware of greed which grows into crime and makes men forget the poor. A man's life should not be for himself, but for his people. For them he must be ready to die.

This is the sum of Native American economic teachings. (Eastman)

CHEERFULNESS

Nothing seems to anger the educated Native, today, more than oft-repeated absurdity that his race was of a gloomy, silent nature. Anyone that has ever been in a village knows what a sense of joy and good cheer it normally was. In every such gathering, there was always at least one recognized fun-maker, who led them all in joke and hilarious jest. Their songs, their speeches, their fairytales are full of fun and dry satire. The reports of the Ethnological Bureau sufficiently set forth these facts.

"The common belief that the Native is stoical, stolid, and sullen, is altogether erroneous. They are really a merry people, good-natured and jocular, usually ready to laugh at an amusing incident or a joke, with a simple mirth that reminds one of children." (Grinnell)

The tribes in general are a place of joy and some merriment and not usually observed by outsiders. People of all nations prefer cheerfulness when given the choice.

OBEDIENCE – REVERENCE FOR THEIR PARENTS AND FOR THE AGED

We cannot, short of the Jewish or the Chinese, perhaps, find more complete respect for their parents than among the Native American.

Among the maxim laid down by the venerable Chief of the Kansas, was:

"Obey and venerate the old people, particularly your parents." (Teachings of Tshut-che-nau, Chief of the Kansas Tribe)

"The Natives always took care of their aged and helpless. It was a rare exception when they did not." (Francis LaFleshe)

KINDNESS

At every first meeting of Native Americans and settlers, the settlers were inferior in numbers, and yet were received with the utmost kindness, until they treacherously betrayed the men who had helped and harbored them. Even Christopher Columbus, blind and burnt up with avarice as he was, and soul-poisoned with superstition, and contempt for an alien race, yet had the fairness to write home to his royal accomplice in crime, the King of Spain:

"I swear to your Majesties that there is not a better people in the world than these; more affectionate, affable or mild. They love their neighbors as themselves, and they always speak smilingly." (Catlin)

"But if they are thus barbarous to those with whom they are at war, they are friendly, hospitable, and humane in peace. It may with truth be said of them, that they are the worst enemies and the best friends of any people in the world." Jonathan Carver

"When Lone Chief had gone into the Lodge of the Chief of the enemy, and food and water had been given to him, the Chief stood up and spoke to his tribespeople saying, 'What can I do? They have eaten of my food, I cannot make war on people who have been eating with me and have also drunk of my water." ("Pawnee Hero Stories")

TREATMENT OF THEIR WOMEN

"The social condition of the North Americans has been greatly misunderstood. The place of women in the tribe was not that of a slave or of a beast of burden. The existence of the gentile organization, in most tribes, with decent in the female line, forbade any such subjugation of women. In many tribes, women took part in the councils of the chiefs; in some, women were even the tribal rulers; while in all, they received a fair measure of respect and affection from those related to them." (Grinnell)

"It has often been asserted that the Native American men did no work, even leaving the cultivation of the corn and squashes to the women. That the women in some tribes tended the crops, is true, but in others, like the Pueblos, they seldom or never touched hoe or spade. The Eastern men were hunting or building boats, or were on the war path, hence it was necessary for the women to look after the fields." (F.S. Dellenbaugh)

Omaha manners:

"Politeness is shown by men and women. Men used to help women and children to alight from horses. When they had to ford streams, the men used to assist them, and sometimes they carried them across on their backs." (Dorsey)

"One of the most erroneous beliefs relating to the status and condition of the Native American women is, that she was, both before and after marriage, abject slave and drudge of the men of her tribe, in general. This view, due largely to inaccurate observation and misconception, was correct, perhaps, at times, as to a small percentage of the tribes and peoples whose social organization was the most elementary kind politically and ceremonially, especially of such tribes as were non-agricultural." (Handbook of American Indians)

"In most, if not in all, the highly-organized tribes, the woman was the sole master of her own body." (Handbook of North American Indians)

"A mother possessed the important authority to forbid her sons going on the war-path, and frequently the chiefs took advantage of this power of the women, to avoid a rupture with another Tribe." (Handbook of North American Indians)

COURTESY AND POLITE BEHAVIOR

There has never been any question of the Native American's politeness. Every observer remarks it. The settler who usurped his domain are immeasurably his inferiors in such matters.

"When persons attend feasts, they extend their hand and return thanks to the giver. So, also, when they receive presents. (Omaha politeness)

"If a man receives a favor and does not manifest his gratitude, they exclaim, 'He does not appreciate the gift; he has no manners!'"

"Mothers teach their children not to pass in front of people if they can avoid it." (Dorsey)

TEEPEE ETIQUETTE – THE UNWRITTEN LAW OF THE LODGE

(Gathered chiefly from observations of actual practice, but in many cases from formal precept)

Be hospitable.

Always assume your guest is tired, cold, and hungry.

Always give your guest the place of honor in the lodge, and at the feast, and serve him in reasonable ways.

Never sit while your guest stands.

Go hungry rather than stint your guest.

If your guest refuses certain food, say nothing; he may be under a vow.

Protect your guest as one of the family; feed his horse, and beat your dogs if they harm his dog.

Do not trouble your guest with many questions about himself; he will tell you what he wishes you to know.

In another man's lodge follow his customs, not your own.

Never worry your host with your troubles.

Always repay calls of courtesy; do not delay.

Give your host a little present on leaving; little presents are little courtesies and never give offence.

Say "Thank you" for every gift, however small.

Compliment your host, even if you strain the facts to do so.

Never walk between persons talking.

Never interrupt persons talking.

Let not the young speak among those much older, unless asked.

Always give place to seniors in entering or leaving the lodge; or anywhere.

Never sit while seniors stand.

Never force your conversation on any one.

Speak softly, especially before your elders, or in presence of strangers.

Never come between any one and the fire.

Do not touch live coals with a steel knife or any sharp steel.

Do not stare at strangers; drop your eyes if they stare hard at you; and this, above all, for women.

The women of the lodge are the keepers of the fire, but the men should help with the heavier sticks.

Always give a word or sign of salute when meeting or passing a friend, or even a stranger, if in a lonely place.

Do not talk to your mother-in-law at any time, or let her talk to you.

Be kind.

Show respect to all men, grovel to none.

Let silence be your motto till duty bids you to speak.

Thank the Great Spirit for each meal.

HONESTY

"I have roamed about, from time to time, during seven or eight years, visiting and associating with some three or four hundred thousand of these people, under an almost infinite variety of circumstances; and under all these circumstances of exposure, no Native ever betrayed me, struck me a blow, or stole from me a shilling's worth of my property, that I am aware of." Catlin

"Among (between) the individuals of some tribes or nations, theft is a crime scarcely known."(Hunter)

There is a story told of Bishop Whipple:

He was leaving his cabin, with its valuable contents, to be gone some months, and sought some way of rendering all robber-proof. His Native guide then said: "Why, Brother, leave it open. Have no fear. There is not a settler man within a hundred miles!"

On the road to a certain large Ojibway village in 1904 I lost a considerable roll of bills. My friend, the settler man in charge, said: "If a Native finds it, you will have it again within an hour; if a settler finds it, you will never see it again, for our people are very weak, when it comes to property matter."

TRUTHFULNESS AND HONOR

"Falsehood they esteem much more mean and contemptible than stealing. The greatest insult that can be offered to a Native, is, to doubt his courage: the next is to doubt his honor or truth!

"Lying as well as stealing, entails loss of character on habitual offenders; and, indeed, a Native of independent feelings and elevated character will hold no kind of interaction with anyone who has been once clearly convicted." (Hunter)

"On all occasions, and at whatever price, the Iroquois spoke the truth, without fear and without hesitation." (Morgan)

"The honor of their tribe, and the welfare of their nation is the first and most predominant emotion of their hearts; and from hence proceed in a great measure all their virtues and vices. Actuated by this, they brave every danger, endure the most exquisite torments, and expire triumphing in their fortitude, not as a personal qualification, but as a national characteristic." (Carver)

In brief, during our chief dealings with the Native Americans, our manners were represented by the border outlaws, the vilest criminals the world has known, absolute fiends; and our Government by educated scoundrels of shameless, heartless, continual greed and treachery.

TEMPERANCE AND SOBRIETY

When the settlers struck into the West with their shameful cargoes of alcohol to tempt the simple savages, it was the beginning of the *Great Degradation*. The leading Natives soon saw what the drink habit meant, and strove in vain to stem the rising current of madness that surely would sweep them to ruin.

About 1795, Tshut-che-nau, chief of the Kansas, did his best to save the youth of his people from the growing vice of the day.

"Drink not the poisonous strong-water of the settlers,' he said, 'it is sent by the Bad Spirit to destroy us."

Catlin writes:

"Every kind of excess is studiously avoided."

"Amongst the wild Natives in this country, there are no beggars—no drunkards—and every man, from a beautiful natural precept, studies to keep his body and mind in such a healthy shape and condition as will, at all times, enable him to use his weapons in self-defense, or struggle for the prize in manly games." (Catlin)

PHYSIQUE

The Native American tribes have been the finest type of physical manhood the world has ever known. None but the best, the picked, the chosen and the trained of the settlers, had any chance with them. Had they not been crushed by overwhelming numbers; the Natives would own the continent today.

Grinnell says:

"The struggle for existence weeded out the weak and the sickly, the slow and the stupid, and created a race physically perfect, and mentally fitted to cope with the conditions which were forced to meet, so long as they were left to themselves."

The Arizona tribes are known to run down a deer by sheer endurance, and every student of southwestern history will remember that Coronado's mounted men were unable to overtake the natives, when in the hill country, such was their speed and activity on foot.

"The moment that man conceived of a perfect body, supple, symmetrical, graceful, and enduring – in that moment he had laid the foundation of a moral life. No man can hope to maintain such a temple of the spirit beyond the period of adolescence, unless he is able to curb his indulgence in the pleasure of the senses. Upon this truth the Native built a rigid system of physical training, a social and moral code that was the law of his life.

"There was aroused in him as a child a high ideal of manly strength and beauty, the attainment of which must depend upon strict temperance in eating and in the sexual relation, together with severe and persistent exercise. He desired to be a worthy link in the generations, and that he might destroy by his weakness that vigor and purity of blood which had been achieved at the cost of so much self-denial by a long line of ancestors.

IN GENERAL

"*They are high-minded and proud: possess a courage equal to every trial, an intrepid valor, the most heroic constancy under torments, and an equanimity which neither misfortunes nor reverses can shake. Toward each other they behave with a natural politeness and attention, entertaining a high respect for the aged, and a consideration for their equals which appears scarcely reconcilable with that freedom and independence of which they are so jealous.*" (Moerus des Sauv)

Long afterward the judicial Morgan in his League of the Iroquois, says:

"*In legislation, in eloquence, in fortitude, and in military sagacity, they had no equals.*

"Crimes and offences were so infrequent, under their social system, that the Iroquois can scarcely be said to have had a criminal code."

"The Native American, born free as the eagle, would not tolerate restraint, would not brook injustice; therefore, the restraint imposed must be manifestly for his benefit, and the government to which he was subjected must be eminently one of kindness, mercy, and absolute justice, without necessarily degenerating into weakness. The Native American despises a liar. The Native American is the most generous of mortals; at all his dances and feasts, the widow and the orphan are the first to be remembered." (Bourke)

"The Native North American, in his native state, is an honest, hospitable, faithful, brave; warlike, cruel, revengeful, relentless – yet honorable – contemplative and religious being. Catlin

Omitting here what he gives elsewhere, that the Native American is clean, virtuous, of splendid physique, a master of woodscraft, and that to many of his best representatives, the above evil adjectives do not apply.

"They were friendly in their dispositions, honest to the most scrupulous degree in their interaction with the European settlers." *"Simply to call these people religious would convey but a faint idea of the deep hue of piety and devotion which pervades their whole conduct. Their honesty in immaculate, and their religion are most uniform and remarkable. They are certainly more like a nation of saints than a horde of savages."* (Captain Bonneville)

The earliest of the Norther American Natives to win immortal fame was the great Mohawk, Hiawatha. Although the Longfellow version of his life is not sound as history, we know that there was such a man; he was a great hero; he stood for peace, brotherhood, and agriculture; and not only united the Five Nations in a Peace League, but made provision for the complete extension of that League to the whole of America.

Pontiac, the Napoleon of his people, Tecumseh, the chevalier Bayard, who was great as warrior and statesman, as well as when he proclaimed the broad truths of humanity; Dull Knife, the Leonidas of the Cheyenne, Chief Joseph, the Xenophon of the Nez Perce, Wabasha, Little Wolf, Pita-Lesharu, Washakie, and a hundred others might be named to demonstrate the Native American progress toward these ideals.

SUMMARY

Who that reads this record can help saying: "If these things be true, then judging by its fruits, the Native American way must be better than ours. Wherein can we claim the better thought or results?"

To answer is not easy. The first purpose was to clear the memory of the Native American,

To compare his way with ours, we must set our best men against his, for there is little difference in our doctrine.

One great difference in our ways is that, like the early Christians, the Native was a Socialist. The tribe owned the ground, the rivers and the game; only personal property was owned by the individual, and even then it was considered a shame to greatly increase. They held that greed grew into crime, and much property made men forget the poor.

Our answer to this is that, without great property, that is power in the hands of one man, most of the great business enterprises of the world could not have been, especially enterprises that required the prompt action impossible in a national commission.

All great steps in national progress have been through some one man, to whom the light came, and to whom our system gave the power to realize his idea.

The Native American's answer is, that all good things would have been established by the nation as it needed them; anything coming sooner comes too soon. The price of a very rich man is many poor ones, and peace of mind is worth more than railways and skyscrapers.

In the Native American life there was no great wealth, so also poverty and starvation were unknown, excepting under the blight of natural disaster, against which no system can insure. Without a thought of shame or mendicancy, the young, in the days of their strength, they were taught and eager to serve.

And how did it work out? Thus: Avarice, said to be the root of all evil, and the dominant characteristic of our race, was unknown among the Natives, indeed it was made impossible by the system they had developed.

These facts are long known to the few are slowly reaching all our people at large, in spite of shameless writers of history, that have done their best to discredit the Native American, and to that end have falsified every page and picture that promised to gain for him a measure of sympathy.

Here are the simple facts of the long struggle between the two races:

There never yet was a massacre of Natives by settlers – and they were many – except in time of peace and made possible by treachery.

There never yet was a Native massacre of settlers except in times of declared war to resist invasion.

There never yet was a Native war but was begun by the settlers violating their solemn treaties, encroaching on Native lands, stealing Native property or murdering their people.

There never yet was a successful campaign of settlers against Natives except when the settlers were in overwhelming numbers, with superior equipment and unlimited resources.

There cannot be the slightest doubt that the Natives were crushed only by force of superior numbers. And had the tribes been united, they might possibly have owned America today.

Finally, a famous Native American fighter of the most desperate period thus summarizes the situation and the character of the dispossessed:

"History can show no parallel to the heroism and fortitude of the Native American's in the two hundred years' fight during which they contested inch by inch the possession of their country against a foe infinitely better equipped, with inexhaustible resources, and in overwhelming numbers. Had they even been equal in numbers, history might have had a very different story to tell." (Gen. Nelson A. Miles)

"I never yet knew a man who studied the Native American or lived among them, without becoming their warm friend and ardent admirer." Professor C.A. Nichols, of the Southwestern University, a deep student of Native American life, said to me, (to Seton) sadly, one day last autumn: *"I am afraid we have stamped out a system that was producing men who, taken all around, were better than ourselves."*

Our soldiers, above all others, have been trained to hate the Natives, and yet the evidence of those that have lived years with this primitive people is, to the same effect as that of the missionaries and travelers, namely, that the high-class Native was brave. He was obedient to authority. He was kind, clean, and reverent. He was provident, unspoiled, hospitable, dignified, courteous, truthful, and honest. He was the soul of honor. He lived a life of temperance and physical culture that he might perfect his body, and so he achieved a splendid physique. He was a wonderful hunter, a master of woodscraft, and a model for outdoor life in this country. He was heroic and picturesque all the time. He knew nothing of forgiveness of sin, but he remembered his Creator all the days of his life, and was in truth one of the finest types of men the world has ever known.

Surely, it is our duty, at least, to do justice to his memory, and that justice shall not fail of reward. For this lost and dying type can help us in many ways that we need, even as he helped us in the past. Have we forgotten that in everything the settler learned of woodscraft, the Native was the teacher? And when at length came the settlers fight for freedom, it was the training he got from the Native Americans that gave him the victory. So again, to fight a different enemy today, he can help us. In our search for the ideal outdoor life, we cannot do better than take this Native, with his reverence and his carefully cultured physique, as a model for the making of men, and as a pattern for our youth to achieve manhood, in the Spartan sense, with the added graces of courtesy, honor and truth.

THE PURPOSE AND LAWS OF WOODSCRAFT

THE NATIVE AMERICAN WAY

THESE ARE A SUMMATION of the ways of the great Native American. This is their high code set down for the growth and guidance for all young people building up their bodies and strengthening their soul according to the Woodscraft ways. May all go forth with seeing eyes, steady hand, muscles that fail not, learning to know the pleasant ways of the woods and be an all-wise master of themselves. No matter the stress, ill-fortune, hardship, wounding of the spirit, may they face all without flinching. With the calm fortitude of the Proven Warrior, rather rejoicing that the Great Spirit has been pleased to send them so noble an occasion to show how fully each one, by his will, is ruler of a great soul in its worthy tabernacle.

Indeed, the thought in our Nation and in the Lodge of Vigil: Our *watchword* is *"Blue Sky."* Under the blue sky, in the sunlight, we seek to live our lives and our thoughts are of "blue sky," for that means "cheer". When there are clouds, we know that the blue sky is ever behind them, and will come again.

Our totem is the white horned-shield, with horns of blue and the four elements of earth, wind, fire, and water. The horns are given to fight, and the shield to ward off trouble, and the four elements to remind us of the path we follow. In these, we symbolize that we are ready for all manner of trial.

Our *war-cry* is "How Kola! How Kola! How Kola! Skunka meneetu Yaooooooo!" (which is the "Hail! Brother," and the wolf, and the howl of the wolf).

Our sign is the closed hand held up, with the little finger and thumb out as horns. Raise the hand so the palm forward to the head, and down, is both a courteous salute and a sign that we are of the Brotherhood. Some also in salute add the word "How," or "Haw."

PRACTICAL APPLICATION

From the original Book of Woodcraft, it is our understanding that the goal was to build a national organization for youth and adults, both female and male, to honor and follow the Native American ways. Through observing nature, camping, and being part of a group, all would learn, develop, and grow.

Whether such an organization is established or not, the program can be beneficial to any who choose to follow the steps to learn and grow.

HOW TO ESTABLISH A TRIBE THE WOODSRAFT WAY

The whole Nation is ruled by *The Great Council*, to which all our Head Chiefs, Rulers, Nobles, and Medicine Men may belong if the Council itself invites them. They are many. They meet once a year, and elect in person:

The High Council of Guidance: Made up of fifteen leaders of the Nation and the Head Chief of all Medicine Lodges. They meet as often as needed to guide the nation. In them is the power to make change and enforce all laws. These sixteen shall elect their own Chief, one of themselves. Seven shall be a sufficient quorum and lawful meeting if duly indicated.

The whole Nation is divided into five *Lodges*:

The Brave: 6 to 10 ½ years of age.

The *Warrior*: 10 ½ to 15 years of age.

The *Minisino*: 15 to 21 years of age.

The *Medicine Lodge:* 21 years of age.

Old Guides: 21 years of age and older

Tribe: Each of the first four Lodges is further grouped into Tribes numbering from 20 to 100 members in each.

Band: Each Tribe is divided into Bands of 6 to 12 members each.

The Medicine Lodge or *Lodge of Old Guides*: This is open to all who have shown a righteous spirit within, love and understand the ways of the woods, are willing to help and who are also voted worthy by the Council of their Medicine Lodge. Nevertheless, the High Council of Guidance may withhold its consent, so the election becomes void.

If besides being Old Guides, they take also the title of Camper, Camp Cook, Camp Doctor, and Gleeman, or Herald, they may become Medicine Men of the Lodge.

Every Tribe needs at least one Old Guide or Medicine Man, who presides over their search for wisdom, their Councils in time of difficulty, helping with his experience and knowledge. The Tribe should meet once a week.

JOINING THE TRIBE

Before being admitted as full member of the Tribe, one must be a candidate for at least one month and complete the following:

Know the laws of the Lodge.

Have slept outdoors three nights without a roof overhead (backyards, roof tops, lean-to, tents allowed).

Be nominated, seconded, and attend activities for a month.

If found worthy, may take the vow.

Standing before the Old Guide or Medicine Man/Women in open Council, he shall be questioned and instructed, so he shall know more fully of the sacred purpose of the Order.

Then the Medicine Man/Women shall say to him, "Is it your serious wish to become a member of the Order of Woodscraft Nation?"

His Answer, "It is!"

"Can any here testify that you have fully qualified, by learning the law of the Lodge, by sleeping out for three nights, and by being found acceptable to the Band you wish to join?

Answer, by a leader who knows, "Yes, O Chief, I can vouch for him."

"You know our laws, we shall take them one by one. Do you promise obedience to the Council?"

Answer, "I do!"

And so, through the twelve laws, whereby he is bound to obedience, courage, cleanliness, abstinence from fire-water, tobacco; and to cherish the Great Spirit's gifts; and to kindness, fair-play, loyalty, silence, reverence, honor.

The Medicine Man/Women then says, "Raise your right hand and say after me, *'I give my word of honor that I will obey the Chief and Council and the laws of my Tribe, and if at any time I fail in my duty, I will appear before the Council, when ordered, and submit without murmuring to its decision.'*"

Now, the Medicine Man/Women pins the badge over the candidate's heart, takes him by the hand, and says, "I receive you into our Tribe. I declare your installation complete, as a member of ....Band in the Tribe. Thus he enters the Tribe and the Order by joining a Band.

NOTE: These are the standard requirements for the various levels. A Tribe may modify them according to their needs as long as all fulfill the same requirements. Requirements that move up the levels are cumulative.

Each Brave will need to start their own journal or notebook to keep track of how they are growing and learning.

The following Tribe Laws, requirements, badges, etc. are also based on the original book. A Tribe may choose its own type and style of recognitions based on their resources. Keep them consistent and easily reproducible so all may participate.

BRAVE

(6 to 10 ½ years of age)

To become a Brave:

» Have served as a faithful member for one month.

» Know thirty signs of Sign Language.

» Know six forest trees.

» Walk a mile in twenty minutes.

» Swim fifty yards.

» Follow a trail a quarter of a mile (no snow) in one hour.

» Know and locate the Big Dipper and the North Star.

» Build and light one fire, using two matches with adult supervision.

» Have slept out six nights (it need not be in succession).

» Plan nutritious balanced meals for one week. Clean up after a meal at home three times.

» Demonstrate four knots.

» Make and post a family emergency plan.

WARRIOR

(10½ to 15 years of age.)

To become a Warrior:

» Demonstrate six elementary first aid skills.

» Know ten forest trees by fruit, leaf and trunk.

» Know fifty signs of Sign Language.

» Light five successive campfires with ten matches (with wildwood material).

» Demonstrate six standard knots.

» Swim one hundred yards.

» Walk three miles in one hour.

» Know and locate the North Star, the two Dippers, and at least three the other constellations.

» Have slept out thirty nights. (Cumulative and it need not be in succession).

» Demonstrate appropriate outdoor attire for all situations.

» Have cooked nine digestible meals outside.

» Have a good record in keeping the Laws of the Order.

MINISINO

(15 to 21 years of age)

To become a Minisino:

» Complete an accredited Wilderness First Aid Course.

» Know one hundred signs of sign Language.

» Know ten constellations.

» Know and identify at least ten local wild birds.

» Know and identify at least fifteen local native wild quadrupeds.

» Know twenty forest trees.

» Know twenty wild flowers.

» Complete an accredited Aquatic Life Saving Course.

» Make a rubbing-stick fire with tools made by himself.

» Light ten successive fires with ten matches in different places.

» Single-paddle a canoe one mile in twenty minutes.

» Tie ten standard knots in a rope.

» Dance any good campfire dance.

» Walk four miles in one hour.

» Be able to make a comfortable, rainproof shelter, and a dry, comfortable bed, also light a fire and cook a meal, including roast meat, potatoes, and fresh bread, with no tools or utensils but a hatchet, pocket knife and what he can make with it.

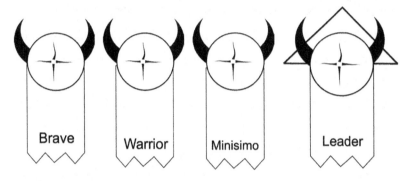

THE LAWS

As set in the original Woodcraft by Seton

Obedience: Obedience is the foundation of all law. Therefore, at all times, obey the law and the Chief and the Council of your Tribe, without evil-speaking or resentment or delay.

Courage: The greatest of all gifts is courage, and the meanest of faults is fear. In the words of Quonab, *"My father taught me there is nothing that can shame a man but being afraid."*

Cleanliness: There is no strength without cleanliness. While the Native American took an ice-cold morning plunge each day, from snow around again to snow, there were none on earth to match them in their strength. But when they fell from this high estate, and forgot the old way, their strength went from them, because with dirt came disease and they became its prey. Foul disease is ever the child of dirt, be it in person, in camp, in speech, or in mind.

Smoking: Let no one use tobacco.

Fire-water: : Let no one use Fire-Water (alcohol).

Wild-life: The Great Spirit made all things, and we have no right to unmake them unless to preserve ourselves. Therefore, protect all songbirds and harmless squirrels. Keep the game-laws, and do no harm to the beauty of the landscape.

Wild-fire: The forest is the father of the rivers and the game. There can be no good thing without the forest. The enemy of the forest is wild fire. At all times, be sure to fight it, and **leave no camp fire unguarded**, lest it should become wildfire.

Kindness: Above all others, the great Tecumseh was kind to every man and to the beasts. And his kindness came again to him. It caused him no loss; no, not the value of a hair, and it gave him power over all men. Let each one strive to do at least one act of kindness every day, for thereby he becomes kinder, and his kindness comes to him again. Do a good turn daily.

Play Fair: Play no game except according to the rules of the game. Loyalty is playing fair; foul play is treachery.

Silence: Do not hasten to speak before your elders. Keep silence in your youth, then it may be your older thoughts will be worth telling.

Reverence: Respect all worship of the Great Spirit and show deference to those that are your elders.

Word of Honor: Word of honor is sacred. Be trustworthy in all things.

THE LAWS FOR THE RULING OF THE TRIBE

1. NAME

This Tribe shall be called "The (any local Native American name or whatever the Tribe decides defines it) Tribe of Woodscraft".

2. PURPOSE

The true purpose of this Tribe and its Councils shall be to learn of the great Native American ways, to seek out and follow the outdoor living life and the pleasures of woodscraft, to work actively for the preservation of wildlife and landscape, to cherish the spirit of Brotherhood and above all, to see the beautiful in all things.

3. WHO MAY ENTER

Those who would enter must show themselves worthy.

Those who would enter must be admitted to a Band of 5 to 10, which is already part of the Tribe, or is afterward made such.

4. COUNCILS

A Council of the Tribe should be held in the first part of each month.

The yearly Council for the election of offices shall be held once a year.

Special Councils may be called by the Chief, and must be called by him upon the written request of one fourth of the Council, or one third of the Tribe.

A quarter of the whole number shall be a quorum of the Council or Tribe.

Seven suns' notice must be given before each Council.

A Brave, Warrior or Minisino may vote at any Council of the Tribe, by proxy in his own handwriting.

5. THE RULERS OF THE TRIBE

Head Chief - elected by the whole Tribe, should be strong and acceptable as the leader, and must enforce the laws. He is Head of the Council and of the Tribe and has charge of the standard which bears the totem of the Tribe.

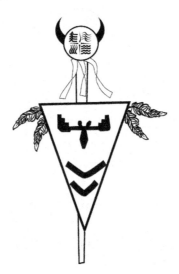

The Second Chief - takes the Head Chief's place in his absence. Otherwise, he is merely a Councilor. He is elected by the whole tribe.

Third Chief - is elected a leader by the whole tribe and only serves when the other two are away.

Wampum Chief or Keeper - is not elected, but appointed for one year by the Chief. He is charged with keeping the money and public property of the Tribe, except the records. He ought to have a lock-box or small trunk to keep valuables in.

Chief of the Painted Robe or Feather Tally - is not elected, but appointed for one year by the Chief. He keeps the tribal records, including the Book of Laws, the roster or roll, the record of camps and activities, and the Feather Tally, or Record of Honors and Exploits. He enters nothing except as commanded by the Council. He should be a bit artistic.

* Sometimes one Councilor or Chief holds more than one office.

The *Old Guide or Medicine Man* - is approved by the whole Tribe and is a member of the   Council.

Add to these the Chief of each Band or Clan in the Tribe, and all the Sachems and Sagamores (See Titles of Nobel's) provided always that that number of non-elective members shall not exceed the number of elective members. These officers and Councilors form the governing body. (If there are too many Nobles, omit those who were latest raised in rank.)

All disputes, etc., are settled by the Chief and the Council. The Council makes the laws and fixes the dues. The Chief enforces the laws.

All leaders are elected or appointed for one year, or until their successors are chosen once a year.

Vow of the Head Chief - (To be signed with his name and totem in the Tally Book.) "I give my word of honor that I will maintain the Laws, see fair play in all activities of the Tribe, and protect the weak."

Vow of each Member - (To be signed with the name and totem of each in the Tally Book.) "I give my word of honor that I will obey the Chief and Council of my Tribe, and if I fail in my duty, I will appear before the Council, when ordered, and summit without murmuring to their fair decision."

6. CHANGES OF THE LAW

Changes of this code may be in harmony with the laws made at any Council by two-thirds vote of all the Tribe.

Notice of proposed amendments shall be made public for at least seven suns before the meeting.

7. DUES

Dues shall be set by each Tribe to be collected in each Band. Assessments may be made by the Council for Tribal expenses.

The new member fee shall include the first year's dues, but this shall not include assessments.

8. CONFIDENTIALITY

Council meeting discussions shall stay a part of the meeting and not to be discussed outside of the light of the council meeting.

THE BAND

Each Band of not less than five or more than ten members, elects its Chief for one year, or until his successor is elected. The Chief appoints his own Second Chief, to act in his absence, and also a Tally Keeper, who should be an artist, for it is his office to keep the records, The Winter Court, and the Tally Robe of his Band, it is his glory to embellish them in all ways. A Wampum Keeper, also is needed, and may be appointed by the Chief, though he, himself may act, unless otherwise arranged. The other members, even those of lowest degree, sit in the Council without election.

Two to fifteen, or even twenty, Bands, unite to form a Tribe. Every member of the Band is a member of the Tribe and he may use the Tribal Totem and Call. But the Band has also a Totem and a Call of its own.

The Band keeps its own Tally, and collects dues as needed. It also pays dues to the Tribe and is represented in the Tribal Council by its Chief and Nobles (if any) and such Tribal Councilors as it can elect. One Medicine Man or Old Guide may serve for the whole Tribe.

REGALIA

The regalia is to be decided on by each Tribal Council according to the local area, terrain, and custom. When choosing, look at what is available in your area. Consider longevity as this will become the traditional uniform of the Tribe. (Native American, Hunter-Trapper, Modern) This "uniform" is worn to all meetings and activities, so choose with care.

TITLES OF NOBLES

When a Brave has won 24 honors, according to the Standard of Honors, he may claim the title of *Sagamore*.

He that has won 36 grand honors becomes a *Grand Sagamore*.

He that has won 48 grand honors becomes a *Grand Sachem*.

All *Sachems* and *Sagamores* sit in Council of their Tribe without election, and by right of their honors.

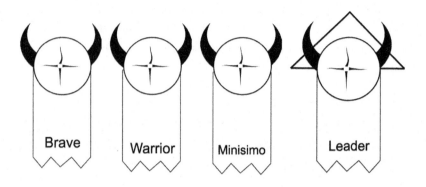

BADGES OF RANK

Each Tribe will establish its own set of badges and how or where they are displayed. Badges should be made simply and with easily available materials and be reproducible. Generally, they are worn on the chest, armband or headband. A sash, shirt, vest, hat, or jacket may also be utilized as long as all in the Tribe are similarly outfitted. Each Tribe will establish its own set of badges and how or where they are displayed.

The badge of the *Brave* is a green ribbon, bearing the blue horned white shield of Woodscraft. It is displayed prominently and proudly.

The badge of the *Warrior* is a blue ribbon, bearing the blue horned white shield of Woodscraft.

The badge of the *Minisino* is a red ribbon, bearing the blue horned white shield of Woodscraft.

** As advancing to the next older age Band, previous titles and degrees are no longer worn. The badges for adults are pictured below. The Tribe chooses where and how these are worn.

The badge of leaders is a yellow ribbon, bearing the blue horned white shield of Woodscraft on a white triangle.

The badge of the Chief is a head-band or arm band with two horns on it, worn in addition to his other badge. (Council may decide on appropriate head gear.)

The badge of the *Old Guide* is the horned-shield on a broad blue band.

The badge of the *Medicine Man* is the same, but with a red band, and on the shield are two eyes, to signify that he is a Seer, whereas, others move in blindness.

The badge of the *Sagamore* is a black and white war bonnet.

The badge of the *Grand Sagamore* is a black and white, tufted war bonnet.

The badge of the *Sachem* is a black and white war bonnet with tail.

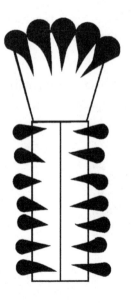 

The badge of the *Grand Sachem* is a black and white tufted war bonnet with two tails. All are worn on the spear arm, or on the breast.

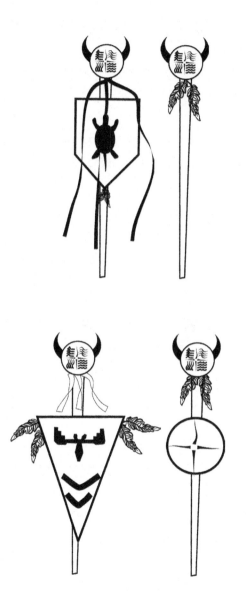

THE STANDARD

The standard of the Tribe or Band is a staff about eight feet long, painted red, and bearing a shield with the totem of the Tribe or Band. A small shield on top is white with blue horns, to typify the whole nation. The standard is carried around when a proclamation is being made. If the Chief deputizes another to be Herald, he also gives him the standard to carry as a badge of authority.

Some Tribes may prefer to carry a banner standard instead of a shield standard in which case the banner is hung on a cross piece.

When not in use, the standard is placed in the ground or a base, near the Chief's teepee, tent, or lodge.

TOTEMS

The Totem of the Whole Nation of Woodscraft is the White Buffalo head, symbolized by the Horned White Shield. This is used chiefly on Totem poles, standards, and in publications.

Each Tribe, of course, has a special Totem. This is selected by the Council, and should be something easy to draw and reproduce. So, also, each Band has its totem and finally, each brave adds a private Totem of his own, usually a drawing of his Native American name or camp name, if he wins one.

As soon as organized, the Tribe or Band should select a Totem and a Call. Take one out of the accompanying list, or a modification of one of them, or take any one that is suggested by members of the Tribe. Frequently, the Tribe name, call, totem, and individual's name will have a special meaning to the group. Thus, you might take the "Wild Cat," but wish to have it of some other color. This you are free to do. Take one, two, three, or even four colors if you like, but two are most convenient for reproduction. Do not be afraid to select other colors, but always keep the colors primary and secondary; avoid mere pictures on the flag.

Any bird, animal, tree, or flower, will do for the Totem, but it is better if it has some special reason. Choose at least two colors and make sure it is simple for all to draw and reproduce.

Some suggestions from the original Woodcraft book:

THE CALL OF THE BAND

The *Call* is something to be carefully considered. Remember the Calls and Totems given here are mere suggestions, you can take one of these or take any other bird, reptile, fish, animal or object that commends itself to you and is easy to draw and imitate.

In many of the Totems suggested, no Call is given. To supply this, use any local yell or call that your fellows can do or invent or make with two sticks, stones, or other apparatus. It might be a rhythm clap with a response or a simple "yippee" type yell.

Some Sample Totems

Light Heart
Red on pale blue

Kingsnake
Yellow, red spots
Pale green ground

Shining Mountain
Dark blue semi-circle
with white mountain

Arrowheads
Turquoise on dark brown

**Flying Patrol
Fleet Foot
Winged Heel**
White on red

War Quill
White feather, black tip
with red tuft on yellow

Blue Sky
Large blue circle
on white

Deerfoot
Yellow and Black
on blue green
Pat-Pat-Pat

Yellow Quill
All yellow with black tip
on pale green

Ojibwa
Orange on Pale Blue
Peace Whoop

Horseshoe
Blue on pale Yellow
Clink-Clank

Seven Stars
Pale pink on dark blue

Red Arrow
Red on white
Zip zip

Snapper Band
Red on turquiose
Snap-ouch

Red Hand
Red on gray
Ho

Black Foot
Black and Red
War Whoop

HOLDING COUNCIL

The Head Chief, or the Herald he may appoint, walks around with the standard, announcing that a Council is to be held, and all must come to Council. Or, the Tribe may choose a regular day and use the Herald for unforeseen circumstances.

Order of The Day

» Roll Call

» Tally of last Council and report of Tally Chief.

» Report of Wampum Chief.

» Reports of Bands.

» Left-over business.

» Complaints.

» Honors awarded.

» New Braves.

» New business.

» Challenges, etc.

» Activities, skills, songs, dances, stories.

» Closing.

HOW TO BUILD A BAND/ ORGANIZE A NEW TRIBE

Suppose that you have a lot of fellows that want to form a Band of Woodscraft. They ought to be a gang that usually goes together, not less than five or more than ten, between ages 6 to 10 ½, 10 ½ to 15, 15 to 21. They should live near each other. It is no use taking in fellows that live in another town. With these you organize a Band.

This is how to go about it: Get a copy of "Woodscraft" from your local book store or off the internet. Read or tell them the first few pages, the Law, and the Life of Tecumseh. Talk it over and see if all are fully inspired with the idea. If they like it, get a couple of suitable adults to act as your Old Guides, which means a person of good character and is able and willing to give the time.

First you will need to look for a Tribe for your Band to join. If none is available or willing to accept your Band, you will need to form two Bands and start a new Tribe.

If a new Tribe is to be established, a group of three to five adults will need to serve as the Medicine Lodge advisors. As soon as the adults have ten to twenty youth and the Bands are formed, the election process for Chief will need to take place.

While the Braves, Warriors, and Minisinos are preparing, at this time you should be thinking of what name the band is to bear. Turn to the pages with Totems and Calls for suggestions. You should use some animal or object that is easy to draw and not already used by a band in your region, preferably one or something that belongs to your area of the country. Do not hesitate to make little changes in the color, etc., of the design if you can make it more acceptable and reproducible.

You may wish to use the Wolf Totem because some of your fellows are good at howling, or the Hoot Owl because your leader has had some good lessons in hooting. For colors take two, three or four if you like, but two is the best combination.

Having organized your Band let them elect for one year a Chief, one of their number, the natural leader of the gang.

Get a blank book with several pages (enough for a year of records) like a composition book or use a 3-ring binder to be the Tally Book of the Band. This book the chief should either keep himself or appoint one of his band to keep. He should also appoint a Wampum Keeper or else take the office himself. As the leader, the chief delegates tasks as much as possible.

THE TALLY / RECORD BOOK AND HOW TO KEEP IT

The Tally Book is the record of the Band's activities. It should be kept like the proceedings of any other society. The Tally Keeper who is an artist has a great advantage, as a few sketches and photographs thrown in make a most interesting variation. This becomes the scrapbook of the Band. This book may be the record of the Band for a year or until it is filled and a new one started.

Some of these Tally Books are beautifully illustrated with colored drawings and are highly prized. In some cases, each member has added his thumb mark in printer's ink opposite his name when first entered or totem.

The first or title page of the Tally Book should bear an inscription thus:

The Tally Book

of the

(Insert Band or Tribe Name Here)

Woodscraft Nation

The next page might say:

On the First activity of the New Year, the following assembled at (Present location) to form a Band of Woodscraft. List names of attendees, with phone numbers, email addresses, and mailing addresses.

Record a bit about all meetings and activities in the Tally Book as well as who attended. Include the date, those in attendance, interesting things that happened, sketches and photographs.

The regular order of business should be followed in all meetings: The Old Guide takes the chair, or in his absence, or at his request, the Chief of the Band takes the chair and the meeting goes as follows:

Roll Call

» Record of last Council and report of Tally Chief

» Report of Wampum Chief

» Reports of Scouts

» Left-over business

» Complaints

» Honors awarded

» New Braves

» New business

» Challenges, etc.

» Activities, skills, songs, dances, stories

» Closing

» Clean up

THE LAWS OF WOODSCRAFT

Obedience is the brave's first duty.

Courage is the brave's highest gift.

Keep yourself and your camp *Clean.*

No *Smoking*

No *Alcohol*

Take care of all harmless *Wild-life.*

Ever guard against *Wild-fire.*

Do at least one *Kindness* every day.

Play Fair. Foul play is treachery.

Keep *Silence* before your elders, unless duty bids you to speak.

Respect all Worship of the *Great Spirit.*

Word of Honor is sacred.

HONORS, DEGREES, AND NATIVE AMERICAN NAMES

HONORS

Honors are either individual or group. Any brave may take both kinds, if he wishes.

The standards for the individual honors are higher.

Always attain parental permission first before attempting any Honors. The buddy system is the preferred method in all cases.

DECORATIONS FOR INDIVIDUAL HONORS

The decorations for Honors are beads and for High Honors are feathers. The Tribe chooses the bead type and color for each

Honor and the type and color of feather for each High Honor. Be sure the beads and feathers are available and easily resourced. Be consistent with the recognitions for all members.

Craft stores and internet suppliers should be part of the decision process for long-term resourcing along with the crafting skills of the leadership and parents.

DECORATIONS FOR GROUP HONORS OR DEGREES

The decorations for the group honors or degrees, of which there are twenty-four, are set forth on the following pages and may be an honor band made in beads, quills, or embroidery. These honor bands are used as arm bands or as decorations. You might also consider a length of rawhide or string that beads and feathers can be displayed on or added to the Band Totem instead of worn by individual members.

STANDARD OF HONORS

These exploits are intended to distinguish those who are outstanding in their Band and those who are so good that they may be considered in the record-making class. They may be called Honors and High Honors as decided by the Council. No one can count both Honor and High Honor, or repeat their honor in the same sector, except for heroism, mountain climbing, and others that are specified as "repeaters," in which each honor is added to that previously worn.

No honors are conferred unless the exploit has been properly witnessed or proven. Honors are allowed according to the standard of the year in which the application was made.

An honor, once fairly won, can never be lost for subsequent failure. Except when otherwise stated, the exploits are meant for all ages. Always attain parental permission first before attempting any Honors. The buddy system is the preferred method in all cases.

Any one counting Honor, according to the class above him may count it a High Honor in his own class, unless otherwise provided.

The Council will gladly consider suggestions, but it must be understood that no local group has any power to add to or vary the exploits in any way whatsoever.

CLASS 1. RED HONORS

Signified by a Red Bead for Honors & a Feather added for High Honor.

It is up to the Woodscrafter to record achievements in their personal Field Journal. These are cumulative skills. Some may require practice to develop the skill. The feeling of accomplishment is worth the effort. Always attain parental permission first before attempting any Honors. The buddy system is the preferred method in all cases.

HEROISM

Honors are allowed for *saving* a human *life* at risk of one's own; it may be an Honor or High Honor, at the discretion of the Council.

Exemplary *Courage* - the measure of which has not yet been discovered.

RIDING

To *ride* a horse 1 mile in 3 minutes, clearing a 4-foot hurdle and an 8-foot water jump – Honor. To do it in 2 minutes, clearing a 5-foot hurdle and a 12-foot water jump - High Honor.

Trick-riding: To pick up one's hat from the ground while at full gallop on a horse of not less than 13 hands - Honor. To do it 3 times without failure, from each side, with horse of at least 15 hands - High Honor.

GENERAL ATHLETICS

Playing a whole season on any local Sports Team - Honor. Placing well in a Competition - High Honor.

Participate a whole year in Martial Arts, Gymnastics, Cheer Leading, etc. earns Honor. Placing well in a Competition - High Honor.

OUTDOOR ACTIVITIES

These may not be appropriate for those under 10 1/2 years old

Sailing: Sail any two-man craft for 5 days, 3 hours at the wheel or tiller (accumulated) – the other man not a professional sailor – Honor. To have sailed any two-man craft for 10 days, 6 hours at the wheel/tiller (accumulated) – the other man not a professional sailor – High Honor.

Paddleboard: Tread a Paddleboard 100 yards in any time, without going overboard - Honor; do it for 100 yards and back in 30 minutes – High Honor.

Canoe: Demonstrate the basic canoe strokes on calm water – Honor. Demonstrate the righting of a spilled canoe – High Honor.

Canoe-camper: A continuous canoe trip of 2 nights, sleeping out both nights – Honor. Make a continuous canoe trip of 50 or more miles over several nights – High Honor.

Saddle-camper: A continuous saddle trip of 2 nights, sleeping out both nights – Honor. Make a continuous saddle trip of 50 or more miles over several nights – High Honor.

Camper: Camp 15 nights (accumulated) out of doors in a tent, teepee, or bivouac every night - Honor. Sleep out 30 nights, (accumulated) including at least 5 nights in a row – High Honor.

Backpacker: Traveling 50 miles on foot with a group, carrying one's own equipment and supplies, sleeping and cooking outdoors – Honor. Traveling for 125 miles carrying one's own equipment and supplies, sleeping and cooking outdoors – High Honor.

Ski: travel 6 miles in an hour, 40 miles in one day, covered 40 feet in a jump, and traveled 100 miles all told – Honor. To have traveled 7 miles in one hour, 50 miles in one day, made a 50-foot jump, and traveled 200 miles in all - High Honor.

MOUNTAIN – CLIMBING

Not open to those under 14)

The exploits in this class are repeaters. The first one to climb a standard peak gets double honors - one for the *climb*, and one for *first climb*.

Note For those over 14 and under 18

TARGET SHOOTING

(Not open to those under 14)

Everything that can be said in favor of firearms for personal use in general sport applies to the instruction and use of all firearms. Instruction on use, care, and safety will be under the supervision of qualified instructor.

Pistol Shot: Target is 4 x 4 ft. Bull's eye is 8 inches (counts 4 points). Inner-ring 2 feet (3 points). Outer ring, the rest of the target (2points). Distance, 30 yards. Ninety-six shots divided in any number up to six days, one hand, standing 250 points - Honor 300 -High Honor. Half with left hand only; half with right only: 230 points - Honor; 260 - High Honor.

Rifleman: To be a *marksman* of the highest rank but one, according to militia standards, - Honor. To be an *expert rifleman* of the highest rank, - High Honor.

OBSERVATION

Sit in one spot and see how many objects you can identify that are 25 yards away – Honor. To identify the same number of objects 25 - 50 yards distant – High Honor.

CLASS II. WHITE HONORS

CAMPERCRAFT

It is up to the Woodscrafter to record achievements in their personal Field Journal.

These are cumulative skills. Some may require practice to develop the skill.

Signified by a White Bead for Honors & a Feather for High Honor. Always attain parental permission first before attempting any Honors. The buddy system is the preferred method in all cases.

Bee-line: Come to camp through strange woods from a point one mile off in 30 minutes – Honor. In 20 minutes – High Honor.

Match-fire: Light 15 campfires in succession with 15 matches, all in different places, all with stuff found in the woods by oneself, and one fire to be lit on a wet day – Honor. If all 15 are done on wet days, or lighting 30, of which two are on wet days – High Honor.

Flint and Steel Fire: To light 15 campfires in succession with wildwood tinder, one at least on a wet day, and none to take over a minute from striking the flint to seeing flames – Honor. If all 15 are done in one day, or if he does 30 fires in unbroken succession, two at least on wet days, and in no case more than half a minute from strike to blaze – High Honor.

Rubbing-stick Fire: Light a fire with a fire-drill or rubbing-sticks, with material of one's own gathering – Honor. To light the fire in one minute – High Honor.

Water Boiling: Boil one quart of water in a 2-quart pail in 11 minutes – Honor. In 9 minutes – High Honor. Allowed one log, one match, one axe or hatchet. The water is boiling when jumping and bubbling all over the surface.

Axeman: Build a safe ax yard. Sharpen a Bow saw, Hand Ax, Full Ax, and Pocket Knife. Saw a six-foot log, at least six inched in diameter log into 24 inch sections. Split the 24 inch sections. Make a Tent Peg and a Fuzz Stick – Honor. Teach proper use of the Bow Saw, Pocket Knife, Hand Ax, and Full Ax to 8 individuals. Teach proper use of woods tools to saw a log into split able lengths, split a log in usable firewood, make a fuzz stick, and tent peg– High Honor.

Knots: To make 10 different standard knots in a rope – Honor. To make 20 - High Honor.

Lasso: To catch 10 horses or cattle in a corral, with 10 throws of the lasso – Honor. To catch 10 on the range in 10 throws – High Honor.

Lasso: To catch a horse or beef by each of his four feet in four successive throws – High Honor.

Lasso: To catch, throw, and "hog-tie" a beef or horse in 2 ½ minutes – Honor. To do this in 1 ½ minutes – High Honor.

Diamond Hitch: Pack a horse with not less than 100 pounds of gear and tied with a diamond hitch that holds securely during 8 hours of travel - Honor. Ten days in succession – High Honor.

Size Guessing: To guess one inch, one foot, one yard, one rod, one acre, 100 yards, 200 yards, one quarter mile, one half mile, and a mile, with 20% accuracy - Honor. Within 10 % of accuracy – High Honor.

Height and Weight Guessing: To guess the height of 10 trees or other high things, and the weight of 10 stones or other things ranging from one once to 100 pounds, within 10 % accuracy - Honor. Within 5 % – High Honor.

Gauging Distance: To measure the height of 10 trees without climbing, or 10 distances across a river, etc., without crossing, within 10 per cent, of average error - Honor; 5 per cent – High Honor. Tools: pocket rule only.

Star Gazing: Know, Locate, and name 10 star groups or constellations – Honor. Know 15 star groups and tell the names and something about at least one star in each – High Honor.

Latitude: Take the latitude from the stars at night with a cart wheel or some home-made instrument 10 times from different points, within one degree of average error – Honor. Do this with one half degree of error – High Honor.

Traveler: Take a correct latitude, longitude, and local time - Honor.

Wilderness First Aid: Complete successfully a Wilderness First Aid Course taught and certified by trained personnel – High Honor.

Life Saving: Completed successfully a Lifesaving course taught and certified by trained personnel – High Honor.

Throwing Life Buoy: *For those under 18*: To throw a ring or life buoy 40 feet landing within 10 feet of the mark – Honor. Throwing the buoy 45 feet within 5 feet of the mark – High Honor. In each case, hit the mark 3 out of 5 times. *For those over 18*: To throw it 55 feet within 10 feet of the mark – Honor. 60 feet within 5 feet of the mark – High Honor. In each case, hit the mark 3 times out of 5.

Boat-builder: Build a boat that will carry two men and that can be paddled, rowed, or sailed by them 6 miles an hour – Honor. 7 miles an hour – High Honor.

Sign Language: To know and use correctly 200 American Sign Language signs – Honor. To know and use correctly 400 signs – High Honor.

Wigwag or Myer Signaling: To know this code and signals, as well as send and receive a message a quarter mile off, at the rate of 10 words a minute - Honor. The same, at a mile, 24 words a minute – High Honor.

Morse Code: To know this code and signaling method, as well as receive a message a quarter mile off, at the rate of 10 words a minute - Honor. The same code, at a mile, 24 words a minute – High Honor.

Trailing: Know and clearly discriminate the tracks of 15 common wild quadrupeds, also trail one for a mile, without the aid of snow - Honor. Similarly, discriminate 30 tracks, and follow 3 miles as before, but for 3 different animals – High Honor.

Cooking: Cook 12 digestible meals for at least three persons, using ordinary camp outfit/equipment - Honor. Cook 21 meals and in addition make good bread (7) each day –

Wilderness Cooking: Make and bake bread, fry fish or meat and bake potatoes or fish without pots or pans - Honor or High Honor, according to merit.

Tent or Teepee: Help make a two-man tent or an 8-foot teepee, or better, make it single handed and set them up. Honor or High Honor, according to merit.

Latrine: To have run for three days a perfect latrine - Honor. To add improvements for safety, privacy, and sanitation – High Honors. (Refer to Leave No Trace for guidance.)

Basket Weaving: To have made a serviceable basket of wildwood materials and not less than 5 inches across – Honor or High Honor, according to merit.

Weaving: To have woven a good rug, square or round, not less than 2 X 5 feet or 3 feet across – Honor or High Honor, according to merit.

Blazes and Signs: Make the 4 usual Native American Signs or Blazes in twigs, grass, stones, give smoke signals – Honor or High Honor, according to merit.

Herald: Open and lead the Council, light the sacred fire, perform a Naming Ceremony. Know three Native American dances and songs. Honor or High Honor, according to merit.

Linguist: Learn a new language and be able to carry on a conversation – High Honor

Dancer: Know four Native dancing songs and can dance each. Teach to 8 individuals – Honor. Preform with those you have taught at a large gathering - High Honor.

Peace Messenger: Know 50 signs of the Sign Language and translate into English from any other language sentences amounting to 100 words - Honor. Know 150 signs and translate from two languages – High Honor.

Indian Clock: Make a Native American clock, that is a sundial, that accurately works for your area - Honor or High Honor, according to merit.

Tomtom: Make and decorate a tomtom - Honor or High Honor, according to merit.

Map: Make a correct map of a region one-mile-long, ¼ mile wide, such as a mile of back road, taking in 1/8 of a mile on each side, marking every house, fence, hill, stream, bridge and prominent tree. Honor or High Honor, according to merit.

Sweat Lodge: Make and use properly a Sweat Lodge three times in one month, in two of the times it may be given to another person - Honor. Run a Sweat Lodge successfully for one month, treating at least a dozen participants – High Honor.

Bow and Arrows: Make a bow and 6 arrows that will carry 100 yards - Honor. A Set that will carry 150 yards – High Honor.

CLASS III. BLUE HONORS

Signified by a Blue Bead for Honors & a Feather for High Honor. Always attain parental permission first before attempting any Honors. The buddy system is the preferred method in all cases.

NATURE STUDY

» Know and name correctly 25 native wild quadrupeds – Honors. Know and name correctly 50 quadrupeds, and tell something about each – High Honors.

» Know and draw unmistakable pictures of 15 tracks of our four-footed animals – Honors. Draw 25 – High Honors.

» Know and name correctly 50 of our native birds as seen mounted in a museum, zoo, or from a photograph. The female and young count separately, when they are wholly different from the male – Honor. 100 birds – High Honor.

» Know and name correctly 50 wild birds in the field – Honors. 100 – High Honors.

» Recognize 50 wild birds by call or song – Honors. 100 calls with something interesting about each – High Honors.

» Know and name 10 turtles – Honors. 20 with something interesting about each – High Honors.

» Know and name 10 different snakes, tell which are poisonous – Honors. 20 – High Honors.

» Know and name 10 different Amphibians – Honors. 20 – High Honors.

» Know and name 25 fish – Honors. 50 – High Honors.

» Know and name 25 native salt-water and fresh-water shells – Honor. 50 – High Honor.

» Know and name 25 butterflies and moths – Honor. 50 – High Honor.

» Know and name 50 other insects – Honor. 100 – High Honor.

» Know and name 25 trees, and tell something interesting about them- Honor. 50 – High Honor.

» Know and name correctly 50 of our wild flowers – Honor. 100 – High Honor.

» Know and name correctly 25 of our native mosses – Honor. 50 – High Honor.

» Know and name correctly 50 common toadstools or mushrooms – Honor.100 – High Honor.

GEOLOGY, ETC.

Paleontology: Know and name, referring to their proper strata, 25 native fossils – Honor. 50 – High Honor.

Mineralogy: Know and name 25 minerals – Honor. 50 – High Honor.

Geology: Know, name and describe the 14 great divisions of the earth's crust. Define watershed, delta, drift, fault, glacier, terrace, stratum, and dip. Identify 10 different kinds of rocks - Honor. Define and identify sedimentary, metamorphic, anticlinal, synclinal, moraine, coal, metal, mineral, petroleum, and identify 20 kinds of rock– High Honor.

PHOTOGRAPHY

Take a good recognizable photograph of any wild bird larger than a robin, while on its nest - Honor. Make a good recognizable photograph in focus of a wild animal in the air – High Honor.

Take a good recognizable photograph of any wild fish or aquatic mammal - Honor. Make a good recognizable photograph in focus of a wild fish or aquatic animal in the air – High Honor.

THE DEGREES OF WOODSCRAFT

These degrees are earned by individuals in Band, Tribe, community or other events or competitions. The degrees may be worn on a shirt, vest, a sash, jacket, or arm band as decided by the Council. Degrees are made locally from Tribe resources. Start with fabric, felt, fun foam, cross stitch fabric, or ribbon. Degrees are one to one and half inches square when finished. Use paints, markers, thread, yarn – whatever your resources – to create your degrees. If someone has embroidery (hand or machine) skills, that may be a good choice, too. Use the resources and skills available to the Tribe, just keep the finished badges consistent. Square degrees will work best for consistency and durability.

ARCHER

The Degree of Archer may be conferred on those who complete all of these tests:

Events marked * are not optional.

1. *State and explain the Range Safety Rules.
2. *Have knowledge of the different kinds of bows and arrows and be able to explain the differences and uses.
3. *Know the parts of the arrow.
4. *Know the parts of the bow.

5. *Make an arrow with tip and fletching.

6. *Be able to hit a 4-foot target from a distance of 30 feet 8 out of 10 times.

ASTRONOMER

The Degree of Astronomer may be conferred on those who take 9 of these tests:

Events marked * are not optional.

1. *Have a general knowledge of the nature and movement of the stars.

2. *Point out and name 10 principal constellations. 6 – Brave.

3. *Can find the North by means of other stars than the Pole Star in case of that star being obscured by clouds.

4. Can tell the hour of the night by the stars and moon.

5. Know and can name 20 of the chief stars. 15 – Brave.

6. Know, name and can point out 3 of the planets. 1 – Brave.

7. Have a general knowledge of the positions and movements of the earth, sun, and moon.

8. Have a general knowledge of tides, eclipses, meteors, comets, sun-spots, and planets.

9. *Take the latitude from the stars with home-made instruments, within 1 degree of error. 2 degrees – Brave.

10. *Make a sundial that works.

11. Visit a Planetarium.

ATHLETE

The Degree of Athlete may be conferred on those who take 5 of these tests.

1. *Know the rules and regulations of two team sports.

2. *Maintain good health habits for health and nutrition.

3. *Create a chart to monitor healthy eating habits.

4. *Play 2 seasons in any sport.

5. *Discuss the traits of good sportsmanship. Tell what role sportsmanship plays in both individual and group athletic activities.

6. Challenge yourself and others to participate in The Presidents Challenge.

CAMPER

The Degree of Camper may be conferred on those who pass 10 of these tests. **Leave No Trace** is to be used here.

Events marked * are not optional.

1. *Can light 15 fires in succession with 15 matches, at different places, one, at least, on a wet day. (10 for Brave)

2. Have put up a 2-man tent alone, ten times for actual service, ready for storms. (5 times for Brave.)

3. Can make the fire with rubbing-sticks or flint & steel of own preparations.

4. Can boil water in 10 minutes with 1 match, 1 log, 1 axe, 1 quart of water in a 2-quart pail (15 in. for Brave.)

5. *Have made a serviceable bedroll, for all seasons and conditions.

6. Have cooked 21 digestible meals with ordinary camp outfits, for at least three persons. (12 meals for Brave)

7. Construct one useful piece of camp equipment of material found at the camp site.

8. Know how to make a raft.

9. *Know how to choose a camp site and how to prepare for rain.

10. *Know how to build a latrine. (See Leave No-Trace)

11. *Know how to dispose of the camp garbage and refuse.

12. *Have slept out 50 nights (no roof but canvas or nylon); not necessarily consecutive nights. (25 for Brave)

13. Have traveled 50 miles, all told, in canoe, on foot, or in saddle, while sleeping out. (25 for Brave)

14. Have had charge of a camp of five or more for six suns (one week) and kept all going in good shape.

CAMP COOK

The Degree of Camp Cook is conferred on those who pass 6 of these tests: **Leave No Trace** is to be used here.

Events marked * are not optional.

1. Can make a good fireplace of wood, of stone, sod, or earth.

2. *Light 15 fires with 15 successive matches, one on a wet day. (10 fires and 10 matches for Brave)

3. *Cook 5 batches of good bread in a Dutch oven. (3 for Brave)

4. Cook 3 batches of good bread without any utensils but a hatchet. (1 for Brave)

5. *Cook 21 digestible meals over campfire for a party of two or more. (12 for Brave)

6. *Boil a quart of water in a 2-quart pail in 10 minutes. (15 for Brave, given 1 match, 1 log, 1 axe.)

7. Cook a meal consisting of baked bread, meat, poultry or fish, potatoes or rice and a vegetable.

8. Have trained a class in cooking; showing and making them do it properly.

CAMP CRAFTSMAN

The Degree of Camp Craftsman may be conferred on those who pass 15 out of these tests:

Events marked * are not optional.

1. Have a knowledge of tanning and curing.

2. *Make and wear your own moccasins.

3. Can dress a saddle, repair traces, stirrup leathers, etc., and know the various parts of harness.

4. *Can patch a garment.

5. *Can make a lace or a button of a leather patch.

6. Make a set of 6 camp chairs and a camp table.

7. Make a waterproof vessel of natural findings.

8. *Demonstrate knowledge of how to repair a broken boat or canoe.

9. *Demonstrate knowledge of tent, fly, and pole repair.

10. Make an axe handle or hoe handle.

11. Make a basket of wildwood materials.

12. *Demonstrate knowledge of outdoor stoves service and repair.

13. *Demonstrate how to safely sharpen, knife, axe, saw.

14. *Distinguish between a rip saw, crosscut, keyhole saw, 2-handed crosscut and show how they are used.

15. *Show the right and wrong way of putting nails into boards, one of which is to be fastened across the other.

16. Make a boat or a canoe.

CAMP MEDIC

The Degree of Camp Medic is conferred on those who pass 15 out of these tests:

Events marked * are not optional.

***Note: Pass a Wilderness First Aid course.

1. *Pass a Wilderness First-Aid Course.

2. Write a statement on the care of the teeth.

3. State a principle to govern in eating, and state in the order of their importance, five rules to govern the care of his health.

4. Be able to tell the difference in the effect of a cold and a hot bath.

5. *Describe the effect of alcohol and tobacco on a young person.

6. Tell how to care for the feet on a hike.

7. Describe the effect of walking as an exercise.

8. Know how to treat sprains.

9. Tell how athletics can be overdone.

10. *State symptoms and treatment of Heat Stroke, Sun Stroke, and Hypothermia.

11. Tell what should be done to a house which has been occupied by a person who has a contagious disease.

12. Tell how they may cooperate with the board of health in preventing disease.

13. Describe the method used in their community in disposing of garbage and the evil effect of flies.

14. *Know how to treat for sunburn.

15. Tell how a city should protect its foods; milk, meat, and exposed foods.

16. Tell how to plan the sanitary care of a camp.

17. State the reason why school children should undergo a medical examination.

18. *Build a Camp First-Aid Kit.

19. *Know poison ivy, sumac, oak, etc., and the proper treatment for cases of poisoning by these.

20. Make, use, and teach others to use the Sweat Lodge.

21. *Have taught a basic class in First-Aid.

CANOE

Events marked * are not optional.

The Canoe Degree may be conferred on those who pass 12 of these tests, 9 - Brave:

1. *Can tie rapidly 6 different useful knots. 4 – Brave.

2. Splice ropes.

3. Know how to use a palm needle.

4. Fling a rope coil.

5. *Row, pole, scull, paddle, and steer a boat and bring a canoe or boat properly alongside and make fast.

6. Can build a boat or a canoe.

7. Can make a paddle and paint it in the fashion of the First Peoples.

8. *Demonstrate knowledge of repairs on an aluminum, fiberglass, plastic or canvas canoe.

9. *Must know the laws of mooring, beaching, caching, or portaging a canoe, also how to sit in it and how to change seats with another when afloat.

10. *Can swim 100 yards. 50 yards – Brave.

11. Can swim 50 feet with shoes, pants and shirt on and tread water for 5 minutes. Can swim 25 feet with shoes, pants and shirt on and tread water for 3 minutes – Brave.

12. *Have paddled (single) a canoe on calm water, 1 mile in 12 minutes. 15 min. - Brave.

13. *Have spilled the canoe and got into her again, and bailed her without help.

14. *Complete a continuous canoe trip of at least 50 miles, sleeping out every night. 25 miles – Brave.

15. Have a knowledge of weather-wisdom and tides.

16. Can state direction by the stars and sun.

17. Can steer by compass.

18. *Have taught a class to handle a canoe.

CEREMONY LEADER

The Degree of Ceremony Leader is conferred on those who pass 8 of these tests. 5 – Brave.

Events marked * are not optional.

1. *Can open and lead the Council.

2. *Light the Sacred Fire with rubbing-sticks.

3. *Know the Peace Pipe Ceremony.

4. Know the ceremony of giving names.

5. *Can sing many songs, alone or as a leader.

6. Can dance, sing and teach at least three dances.

7. Can tell many stories.

8. And know the art of choosing others to help in the program

9. Know how to welcome new members to the Tribe.

10. Know how to properly end the program.

11. *Teach someone else to run the Council.

FIRE GUIDE

The Degree of Fire Guide may be conferred on those who take 14 of these tests:

Events marked * are not optional.

Not For Brave.

****NOTE****

Contact your local Fire Fighter Association for a Mentor, before beginning this Degree.

1. *Know how to turn in an alarm for fire.

2. *Know how to prevent the spread of fire.

3. Understand the use of hose; unrolling, joining up, connecting two hydrants, use of nozzles, etc.

4. Understand the use of escapes, ladders, and chutes.

5. Know how to improvise ropes and nets.

6. *Know what to do in case of panic.

7. Understand the fireman's lift and drag.

8. How to work in fumes.

9. Understand the use of fire extinguishers.

10. How to rescue animals.

11. How to save property.

12. How to organize a bucket brigade.

13. How to aid the police in keeping back crowds.

14. How to ride a wheel.

15. *Repair a puncture.

16. *Walk 4 miles in one hour.

FISHING

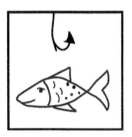

The Degree of Fishing may be conferred on those who pass 8 of these tests, 6 – Brave.

Events marked * are not optional.

1. *Catch and name 10 different species of fish. 7 – Brave. If possible, provide photo evidence.

2. Make a bait rod of 2 joints, straight and sound. Or make a jointed fly-rod.

3. Name and describe 25 different species of fish found in North American waters. 15 – Brave.

4. Give the history of the young of any species of wild fish from the time of hatching until adult stage is reached.

5. Make a net and catch a fish in it.

6. Make a turtle trap and catch a turtle in it.

7. *Make a 6-foot leader with smooth knots to stand a strain of 5 lbs.

8. *Catch, land, and release a fish using a fly-rod. If possible, provide photo evidence.

9. *Catch, land, and release a fish using a rod and reel. If possible, provide photo evidence.

10. Demonstrate the tying of two flies used in your local area.

11. Demonstrate the build of a top-water lure used in your local area.

12. *Build a tacklebox and stock it.

FORESTER

The Degree of Forester may be conferred on those who pass 15 of these tests, 10 – Brave.

Events marked * are not optional.

1. *Can identify 25 kinds of trees. 15 – Brave.

2. Identify 12 kinds of shrubs. 8 – Brave.

3. Collect and identify samples of 15 kinds of wood and be able to tell some of their uses and peculiar properties. 7 – Brave.

4. Determine the height, and estimate the amount of timber, approximately, in 5 trees of different sizes.

5. *Can state the laws for transplanting, grafting, spraying, and protecting trees.

6. Make a collection of 30 species of wild flowers, ferns, or grasses dried and mounted in a book and correctly named. 15 – Brave.

7. *Can recognize in the forest all important commercial trees.

8. Can recognize the difference in the forest between good and bad logging, giving reasons why one is good and another bad.

9. Can tell whether a tree is dying from injury by lightning, fire, insects, disease, age or by a combination of these causes.

10. Knows what tools to use in lumbering.

11. *Knows how to fight fires in hilly or in flat country.

12. Knows the effect upon stream-flow of the destruction of forests at head waters.

13. Knows what are the 4 great uses of water in streams.

14. Knows what causes the pollution of streams, and how it can best be stopped.

15. Knows how, in general, how waterpower is developed.

16. Can tell, for a given piece of farm land, whether it is best suited for use as a farm or forest, and why.

17. Can point out examples of erosion, and tell how to stop it.

18. Can estimate closely how much timber and how much cordwood is in a given acre of woods.

19. Name 6 trees that will float when green, and 6 that will not. 3 & 3 – Brave.

20. *Know something of the relation of birds and quadrupeds to forest trees.

21. Participate in a reforesting project.

22. Have taught a class the rudiments in forestry.

FRONTIERSMAN

The Degree of Frontiersman may be conferred on those who pass 8. 5 – Brave.

Events marked * are not optional.

1. *Plant edible garden of 10 plants. 5 - Brave.

2. *Interpret 15 trail signs. 10 – Brave.

3. Lay a proper camp fire, using all safety concerns and methods.

4. Learn how to weld two pieces of steel together.

5. Make and temper a knife.

6. Know how to find and sanitize drinking water.

7. *Complete a Hunters Safety Class.

8. Show proficiency in tying 6 kinds of knots. 4 – Brave.

9. Lash together a useful piece of camp equipment.

10. Use an axe correctly.

HERALD

The Degree of Herald is conferred on those who take10 of these tests:

Events marked * are not optional.

1. *Can walk 1 mile in 11 minutes. 15 minutes – Brave.

2. Can run 100 yds. In 13 seconds. 15 seconds – Brave.

3. Can run 1 mile in 6 minutes. Not for Brave.

4. Can swim 100 yards.

5. Have slept out 30 nights, cumulative.

6. Can send and receive a message in one of the following systems of signaling: Semaphore, Morse, or Myer, not fewer than 24 letters per minute. 12 letters per minute – Brave.

7. *Can talk Sign Talk, knowing at least 400 signs. 200 signs – Brave.

8. *Know the 25 signs of the First Peoples Code. 15 signs – Brave.

9. *Can read and translate into his own language a page or conversion from some other language.

10. *Can conduct a Council.

11. *Know the ordinary rules of courtesy, precedence, introduction, salutation, etc.

12. Know the history of the National Flag and the proper way of saluting, etc.

13. Teach a dozen members to qualify for this Degree.

HORSEMAN

The Degree of Horseman may be conferred on those who take 10 of these tests:

Events marked * are not optional.

1. *Show that they are at home in a saddle and can ride at a walk, trot, and a gallop.

2. *Know how to saddle and bridle a horse correctly.

3. Can catch 6 horses in corral or on range with 12 throws of the lasso.

4. Know how to water and feed and to what amount and how to groom a horse properly.

5. Know how to harness a horse correctly in single or double harness and to drive.

6. *Can pack 100 lbs. of gear with diamond hitch, to stay during 4 hours of travel. 2 hours – Brave.

7. Have knowledge of the power of endurance of horses at work.

8. Know the management and care of horses.

9. *Can identify unsoundness and blemishes.

10. Know how to check for ill-fitting harness or saddlery.

11. Know two common causes of, and proper remedies for, lameness, and know to whom he should refer cases of cruelty and abuse.

12. Are able to judge as to the weight, height, and age of horses.

13. Know 3 breeds and their general characteristics.

14. Able to treat a horse for colic.

15. Describe symptoms and give treatment for the following: wounds, fractures and sprains, exhaustion, choking, lameness.

16. Understand horseshoeing.

17. *Can clear a 4-foot hurtle and an 8-foot water jump.

18. Pick up their hat from the ground going at full gallop on a horse not less than 13 hands high. 11 hands – Brave.

HUNTER

The Degree of Hunter may be conferred on those who take 14 of these tests:

Events marked * are not optional.

1. Can walk 1 mile in 11 minutes. 14 – Brave.

2. Can run 100 yards in 15 seconds. 20 – Brave.

3. Can run 1 mile in 6 minutes. Not open to Brave.

4. Can swim 100 yards.

5. Can spot, sketch / photograph any animal at 60 yards or more.

6. Can see and map out 6 Pleiades.

7. Can see the Pappoose on the Squaw's back (spectacles allowed if habitually worn.)

8. *Have skillfully tracked and located three animals of different species.

9. *Photograph of a big game animal wild in its native surroundings.

10. *Know and name correctly 25 native wild quadrupeds. 15 – Brave.

11. Know and name correctly 20 wild birds in the field and their nests. 10 – Brave.

12. *Know and clearly discriminate the tracks of 20 of our common wild quadrupeds. 10 – Brave.

13. Can trail an animal or else iron track prints for a half a mile without the aid of snow. Snow allowed for Brave.

14. Have won honors with rifle. That is, be a marks man according to the rules of the National Rifle Association.

15. With bow make a total score of 300 points at 60 yards, standard target. 25 points – Brave.

16. *Have caught alive and uninjured with his own make of trap one wild quadruped and one wild bird.

17. *Know the Pole Star and 10 constellations. 5 constellations – Brave.

18. *Teach any one of these but the first 9 to another.

MOUNTAINER

The Degree of Mountaineer may be conferred on those who take 8 of these tests:

Events marked * are not optional.

1. *Take two honors in the list of mountain climbing. 1 – Brave.

2. Have camped out at least 15 nights in the mountains.

3. Know, name and describe the 14 great divisions of the earth's crust. 8 – Brave.

4. *Know and name 25 different kinds of rock. 10 – Brave.

5. *Define watershed, delta, drift, fault, glacier, terrace, stratum, dip. 5 – Brave.

6. Know at least 20 mammals that live in the mountains. 12 – Brave.

7. Know at least 25 mountain birds. 15 – Brave.

8. Know at least 10 mountain trees. 5 – Brave.

9. Can swim 100 yards.

PATHFINDER

The Degree of Pathfinder may be conferred on those who take 12 of these tests:

Events marked * are not optional.

1. *Know every land bypath and short cut for a distance of at least 2 miles in every direction around your local headquarters in the country. 1 mile – Brave.

2. *Have a general knowledge of the district within a 5-mile radius of his local headquarters, so as to be able to guide people at any time, by day or night. 2 miles – Brave.

3. Know the general direction and population of the 5 principal neighboring towns and be able to give strangers correct directions how to reach them.

4. Know the country in 2-mile radius, or in a town must know in a 1/2-mile radius the Police Station, Fire Station, Hospital, Library are located. 1 mile – Brave.

5. Know the location of the nearest, bakeries, groceries, and drug stores.

6. *Know where the nearest police station, hospital, doctor, fire alarm, fire hydrant, telegraph and telephone offices, and railroad stations are.

7. *Know something of the history of the place, its principle public buildings, such as town hall, post office, schools, and churches.

8. As much as possible of the above information should be entered on a large scale map.

9. Fell a 6-inch tree or pole in a prescribed direction so it falls between two stakes 2 feet apart. Not for Brave.

10. Tie 6 kinds of knots quickly. 4 – Brave.

11. Lash spars properly together for scaffolding.

12. *Build a modern bridge or derrick.

13. Make a camp kitchen.

14. Build a shack or cabin of one kind or another suitable for three occupants.

15. Walk 1 mile in 15 minutes. 20 – Brave.

16. Swim 100 Yards.

RUNNER

The Degree of Runner may be conferred on those who take 9 of these tests:

Events marked * are not optional.

1. *Can walk 1 mile in 15 minutes. 20 – Brave.

2. *Can walk 30 miles in 12 hours. Not open to Brave.

3. Can run 100 yards in 13 seconds. Not open to Brave.

4. Can run 50 yards in 7 4/5 seconds. Not open to Brave.

5. *Can run 1 mile in 5 1/3 minutes. Not open to Brave.

6. *Can swim 100 yards.

7. *Can paddle a canoe 1 mile in 12 minutes. 15 – Brave.

8. 8. Know Semaphore or Wigwag or Myer code and take as well as receive a message at the rate of at least 24 letters a minute.

9. *Know 200 signs of the Sign Language. 100 – Brave.

10. Know the 25 secret signs of the First Peoples Code. 15 – Brave.

11. *Have slept out 30 nights, cumulative.

12. Know and can clearly discriminate the track of 25 of our common wild quadrupeds; trail for a mile without snow, till near enough to photograph. Snow allowed – Brave.

SHARPSHOOTER

The Degree of Sharpshooter may be conferred on those who take 7 of these tests:

Events marked * are not optional.

1. *Qualify as in "marksman" with the rifle in accordance with the regulations of the National Rifle Association.

2. *Make a bow and arrow which will shoot a distance of 100 feet with fair precision.

3. Make a regulation archery target – 4 feet across, with the 9-inch center and 4 rings, each 4 ¾ inches wide.

4. Make total score of 350 with 60 shots of the bow and arrow in one or two meets, using standard 4-foot target at 40 yards or 3-foot target at 30 yards. 300 – Brave.

5. Make a total score of 300 with 72 arrows, using standard 4-foot target at a distance of 50 yards, or 3-foot target at 36 yards. 250 – Brave.

SWIMMER

The Degree of Swimmer may be conferred on those who take 8 of these tests:

Events marked * are not optional.

1. *Can swim 100 yards.

2. Swim on the back 50 feet. 25 – Brave.

3. *Swim 50 feet with shoes and clothes on. 25 – Brave.

4. *Demonstrate breast, free style, back, and side stroke.

5. Dive properly from the surface of the water.

6. Can surface dive in 12 feet of water and bring from the bottom to surface a dive stick, coin, etc. 8 feet of water - Brave.

7. *Demonstrate on land five methods of release from a drowning person who clutches you.

8. Demonstrate in the water two methods of release.

9. Demonstrate resuscitation (CPR).

10. Demonstrate safely crossing thin or rotten ice.

11. Have a knowledge of weather and tides.

12. Teach 3 members to swim.

TRAVELER

The Degree of Traveler may be conferred on those who take 11 of these tests:

Events marked * are not optional.

1. Have walked 1 mile in 15 minutes. 20 – Brave.
2. *Have hiked 20 miles a day. Not open to Brave.
3. Have hiked two different mountain trails.
4. Know at least 15 constellations, including the Dipper and the Little Bear. 10 – Brave.
5. *Have camped out in at least 10 different places.
6. Can take exact latitude and longitude with instruments.
7. Know how to read and follow a road map.
8. Know how to enter and follow GPS coordinates.
9. *Can take latitude within 2 degrees of error, with home-made instruments.
10. Have made a compass survey of 10 miles of country.
11. Have traveled at least 1000 miles by rail, car, air, ship or other means.
12. *Have traveled 50 miles on foot, by bicycle, by canoe, or in saddle, camping out.

13. Know 100 signs of the Sign Language. 50 - Brave

14. Able to make a comfortable bed anywhere traveled.

15. Can swim 100 yards.

16. Have slept out 30 nights, cumulative.

WISE WOODSMAN

The Degree of Wise Woodsman may be conferred on those who take 12 of these tests:

Events marked * are not optional.

1. *Have a list of 25 different kinds of birds observed in the field. 15 – Brave.

2. Identified by sight or song, 25 different kinds of birds in one day. 15 – Brave.

3. Make a clear photograph of 5 wild birds. 3 – Brave.

4. Have secured at least two tenants in bird boxes erected by himself. 1 – Brave.

5. Have daily notes on the nesting of a pair of wild birds from the time the first egg is laid until the young have left the nest. Daily notes 20 to the month – Brave.

6. Have attracted at least 3 kinds of birds, to a self-made bird feeder

7. *Have knowledge of the game laws of the state in which he lives.

8. Mount for a rug the pelt of some fur animal.

9. *Know 25 different kinds of trees. 15 – Brave.

10. *Know 20 different wild flowers. 10 – Brave.

11. Know 10 different snakes. 5 – Brave.

12. Know 10 different fungi. 5 – Brave.

13. Know the signs of weather.

14. Make a fire with the rubbing sticks.

WOODSCRAFT

The Degree of Woodcrafts may be conferred on those who take 9 of these tests:

Events marked * are not optional.

1. Take and print photographs of 12 separate subjects, 3 interiors, 3 portraits, 3 landscapes, and 3 instantaneous "action photos."

2. *Make a recognizable photograph of any wild bird, while on its nest.

3. *Make a recognizable photograph of a wild animal.

4. Make a recognizable photograph of a fish in the water.

5. *Map correctly the country itself the main features of half a mile of road.

6. *Measure the height of a tree, telegraph pole, and church steeple without climbing.

7. Measure width of a river without crossing.

8. Estimate distance apart of two objects a known distance away and unapproachable, within an average of 10 percent of error in 10 different trials.

9. Can measure a gradient.

10. Can estimate the speed of a stream.

11. Can tell the number of gallons of water going over a fall or down a stream.

12. Can estimate the horsepower of a given fall.

13. Teach the last seven to someone else.

Brave - may take three of the first six and three of the second – that is, six in all.

NAMING

Each brave wants a name of their own. The Native names are given in recognition of some exploit, skill, or personal gift. Thus, Deerfoot was the great runner and Hawkeye had sharp eyes. Killdeer was famous in our deer hunt, as also was Deerslayer; Grey-wolf was the best scout; Eel-scout was the one who slipped through the enemies' lines as often as he pleased; Little Beaver was the best worker.

When a name is given, earned from an honor, skill, adventure or life experience. The Chief makes a speech, telling of the exploit and announcing the name. It is written down in the Tally; then each Chief and Councilor comes forward, shakes hands with the brave, saying the new name.

NATIVE NAMES THAT HAVE BEEN USED

As a rule, the idea – "wonderful," "great," "admirable," or "above others" – is understood, or else the name would not have been given.

Native American Names

Anoli – Actor.

Apenimon - Trusty.

Apenindis – Self-reliant.

Ay-no-keetch – Hunter.

Bebe-ji – Wild Horse.

Bedajim – (He) brings the news.

Beejee-gash – Leaping Panther.

Bemossed – Walker.

Biminak – Slick Roper.

Bisanabi – The Silent One.

Bissanajib – Rock-splitter or crusher.

Bodaway – (He) makes fire.

Chissakid – Juggler.

Eesta-nax – Jack Rabit.

Fet-su-moot-si – Brave all alone.

En-do-ban-uh – Scout.

Etut-botsots – Strong alone.

Gash-wan – High Hop.

Gibodeg – Little Breeches.

Giga nini – Man-fish.

Gimab – Spy.

Gimo-gash – Silent power.

Gitch-amik – Mighty beaver.

Gitchi-saka – Big Stick.

Gwaia-koose – He walks straight.

Huya – Fighting Eagle.

Ininaja – (He) was sent.

Ishka-kid – Fire-juggler.

Ishkotekay – (He) makes fire.

Iss-see-kas – Top of the Mountain.

Jangened – Hostile.

Jibendam – Stay with it.

Ka-ba-to – Runner.

Ka-gi-git – Speak not.

Kah-no-see-tuk – Pine Tree.

Kak-ino-sit – The tall one.

Karonawa – Famous Runner.

Kawin-jag – Fears not.

Kee-mo- Sah-bee – Trusty Scout.

Kee-shee Ka-ba-too – Quick Runner

Kijika – (I) walk quickly.

Kin-a-pik – Snake.

Kinji-gisiss – Shinning face.

Manij-wa – Scalper.

Mash-kiki – Doctor.

Me-et-ees – Lone tree.

Mingan – Grey-wolf; that is, "Peerless Scout."

Minikwa or Nita-anoki – Tumbler.

Minobi – (I) an happy.

Minoday – Well cooked.

Minoway – Moving Voice.

Misatik – Big Stick.

Mishe-gash – Mighty Jumper.

Mit-te-gwab – Bow

Mojag – Never Quit.

Neetah Wass-wa – Good Spearman.

Nibaw – I stand up.

Nibenab or Nibab – Sits up all night.

Nibe-jomini – Camp of Creepers

Nita-bimossed – Good Walker.

Nodin – Wind.

Nokidee – Soft Heart.

Nokisan – Wonder Cook.

Odagoma – Iron Nerve.

Okemahgansis – A Little Chief.

Oma-gash – Bounding Buck.

On-jima – Strong Hand.

Ooita-eish – Little Iron.

Osh-ki-de – New Spirit within.

Pajigwad – Stick to it.

Pangi-Wendigo – Little Giant.

Panossim – Water-dog or Sea-dog.

Paw-pung-is – Jumping-jack.

Pe-hask-a – Yellow Hair.

Pee-mah-ta-ha-che-gay – Trailer.

Mee-mah-te-gay – Swimmer.

Pis-chig-ay – Spear.

Shingebis – Diver.

Skunka-reela – Swift or Flying Fox.

So-kit-tay – Strongheart.

Songan – Strong.

So-tee-ay-mo – Brave.

Tchi-bak-we – Medicine Cook.

Wabang – Tomorrow.

Wa-bee-no-sa – Walks all night.

Wadjepi – Nimble.

Wah-bit – Keen Eyes.

Wah-da-ga Swimmer.

Wah-peh-soos – He jumps like a deer.

Wapoos – Rabbit.

Wass-wa Spearman, or Big Spearman.

Agokay – I stick to it.

Anang – Star

Anangons – Little Star

Anohom – Singer

Awashonks, The Women Chief of Seconsit, R.I. 1671

Bimodon – A Grumbler

Gash-kit-on – I am a Winner

Gijig – Sky

Gamowini – Sweet Singer

Kis-ke-mas – Waving Grass

Mijakwad – Skyblue

Minoway – Magic Voice

Mokatewis – Sunburnt

Namid-Anang – Star Dancer

Namid – Dancer

Nijanang – Twin Stars

Niji-Namid – Star Dancer

Ogin – Rose

O-jisoh – A Star

Osawi – Yellow

Osawindibe – Yellow Hair

Pagwadgi – Wild thing

Pingosh – Stinger

Pippinshaas – Bird

Satinka – Magic Dancer

Uppishau – Flower

Wabigoon – White Flower

Wabisi – White Swan

Wap-o – Sunbeam (happiness)

Wetamoo, the beautiful Women

Winne-taska – Pleasant Laughter

Wohsum-Naab – Shinning Eyes

Wohsumoe - Shinning

English Names that Have Been Given

Arrowfoot	Hawk-eye
Bald Eagle	High-hop
Black Hawk	Hoot-owl
Big Moose	Jack-rabbit
Big Otter	Jumping-jack
Deerblinder	Krag
Deerslayer	Leaping Panther
Eagle-eye	Little Thunder
Eel-Scout	Many-tongues
Mustang	Spear-deep
Never-scare	Stongbow
Night-owl	Strongheart
Plenty-coups	Twinklefoot
Red Arrow	White Thunderbolt
Redjacket	Wing-foot
Spy-catcher	Wolverine
Sheet-lightning	

SUGGESTED PROGRAMS

It is recommended the Council chooses a monthly theme and tries to plan a year in advance.

Here are some suggestions for a Monthly Series:

January, the Snow Moon

Outdoors:

» Tracks in the outdoors.

» Gather mosses in the woods for home study.

» Take a bird census.

» Look for cocoons and dormant insects.

» Dig out borers in dead timber for home study.

Indoors:

» Make a target.

» Make a Native American bonnet or head adornment.

» Study Sign Language, picture-writing, wig- wag; knots, splices.

» Learn compass signs.

» Qualify in First Aid.

February, the Hunger Moon

Outdoors:

» Snowshoeing and skiing.

» Prepare emergency food.

» Go to every tree and study the causes of the scars on its trunk; each one is full of history.

» Study, remove, cut and stack, dead trees.

» Play the game "Watching by the Trail."

Indoors:

» Make a Ribbon Shirt.

» Make a beaded flint and steel bag.

» Make Native American furniture.

» Study signaling by semaphore, Myer, Morse, etc.

» Study stone, grass, and stick signs.

» Hand wrestling.

March, the Waking Moon

Outdoors:

» Practice the erecting of tents in all kinds of weather.

» Cut wood for bow and arrows.

» Study geology.

» Take a bird census.

» Track and Trail animals in the local area.

» Make a quiver of canvas or leather.

Indoors:

» Make repairs on camp equipment.

» Make bird boxes to sell.

» Make rustic furniture.

» Make a wooden buffalo skull.

April, the Green Grass Moon

Outdoors:

» Note spring birds' arrivals.

» Collect spring flowers.

» Note early butterflies.

» Do your half-mile work with tracking iron's.

» Make your four-mile walk for degrees.

Indoors:

» One-legged chicken fights.

» Make tracking irons.

» Make a pair of moccasins.

» Learn or create a new Tribal song or dance.

May, the Planting Moon

Outdoors:

» Make a collection of wild flowers.

» Take first over-night hikes.

» Nature compass signs.

» Begin sleeping out your 30 nights.

Indoors:

» Make a 4-foot target for archery.

» Study Wilderness First Aid.

» Study local snakes. Make chart.

» Start seeds for family garden.

June, the Rose Moon

Outdoors:

Fishing, swimming, Native signs.

Practice judging distances.

Learn ten trees.

Indoors:

» Invite new members.

» Study camp hygiene.

» Make a Navaho loom and use it.

July, the Thunder Moon

Outdoors:

» Camping, canoeing, or hiking.

» Play scout messenger.

» Make a sweat lodge.

» Boil water against time, given only one match, log, pail, and a quart of water.

Indoor:

» Learn water purification methods.

» Learn the history of Tecumseh, Dull Knife and others. Tell their stories.

» Plan camp menus, using local sustainable food.

» Study signs of Heat Stoke & Heat Exhaustion.

August, the Red Moon

Outdoors:

» Camping, canoeing, or hiking.

» Water sports.

» Camp Medley - each in turn being called on to dance, sing, tell a story, produce the leaf of a given tree, imitate some animal, or do the four-medley race namely, row a hundred yards, swim a hundred yards, walk a hundred yards and run a hundred, for honors.

Indoors:

» Make dancing and ceremonial paraphernalia.

» Make a hunter's lamp. (Can be solar)

» Clean the indoor meeting area. Evaluate, Remove, Replace.

September, the Hunting Moon

Outdoors:

» Camping, overnight hikes, etc.

» Plan an Equinox Celebration.

» Plan an Honors weekend.

Indoors:

» Make a collection of spore prints, and portraits of fungus.

» When raining: Practice tribal calls, storytelling, and games like Rattler and Feather-blow.

» Make a Peace Pipe of wood.

October, the Leaf-falling Moon

Outdoors:

» Make a collection of leaves and study trees.

» Make a collection of nuts.

» Gather wood for bows and arrows.

Indoors:

» Arrange, mount, and name specimens.

» Learn knots.

» First Aid.

November, the Mad Moon

Outdoors:

» This is the Moon of Short Hikes.

» Plan a winter camping trip.

» Study evergreens.

» Study fire lighting; try a rubbing-stick fire.

Indoors:

» Study Sign Language and picture writing.

» Carve horns, spoons, and cups, decorating with record pictography.

» Research cold weather camping equipment and clothing.

» Decorate the Tally Book.

December, the Long Night Moon

Outdoors:

» Learn the stars.

» Study evergreens.

» Make a collection of twigs and cones.

» Go on a day hike and cook a hot trail lunch.

Indoors:

» Make bead work for costumes.

» Plan and execute fund raising to fund programs.

» Make a Native American Pow-Wow, or Wild-West Show.

» Learn the Native dances.

ORDER FOR WEEKLY MEETINGS

Gathering Activity – this time may be used to instruct new members, if need be, in knots and the laws, or prepare others for Honor and High Honor recognitions.

Roll call & Collect Dues -

Skills Development - Lessons in any of the following subjects like:

» Animals

» Basketry

» Bed-making

» Birds

» Box-making

» Carving

- » Fire Building
- » Fire-lighting
- » Learn a song
- » Lessons in Native Dances
- » Myer or other code
- » Semaphore
- » Stars
- » Sign Language
- » Stars
- » Tell a story
- » Tracking and Trailing
- » Trees

Play a Game

Closing and a Motivational Thought -

Clean-Up –

INDOOR ACTIVITIES

Indoor activities should support the monthly theme and outdoor program. All activities should be based on skill of the individuals and materials available. Here are some ideas:

Carve a *fork* and a *spoon* out of wood, with the band totem on the handle.

Make a *needle case* out of a fowl's leg or wing bone, thus: Clean and smooth about three inches of the bone plug up one end with a soft plug and make a, wooden stopper for the other end. Then with the point of a knife decorate the bone. The lines should be scratched in deeply and then have black paint rubbed into them. If no black paint is handy make a mixture of soot and pine gum, with a little grease, butter or oil.

Make a tackle box or ditty box 2 X 2 X 6 inches carved out of solid wood.

Make peach-stone baskets, of a peach-stone shaped with a file.

Make a Turkey call: An interesting curio is the turkey call. Take a small cigar box and cut off the end. Get a piece of slate about 2 X 3 inches long, or, failing slate, take a flat piece of wood and rub it well with rosin. Draw the two cured edges of the box lightly up this one way, and it will make a wonderfully good imitation of a turkey call.

Make a *Chicken squawk*: This is another call easily made. Take any small round can and make a hole through the bottom and into this put a cord. A knot on the inside prevents the cord from slipping through. Rosin the cord and draw the fingers down it with short and long jerks. This gives a good imitation of a cackling hen.

Picture frames can be made from a variety of materials like sticks, cereal boxes, scrap wood, etc. Use them to frame photographs, certificates, and artwork.

WEEKEND CAMP ROUTINE

6:30 A.M.	Turn out, bathe, etc.
7:00 A.M.	Breakfast.
8:00 A.M.	Air bedding, in sun, if possible.
8:15 A.M.	Business Council of Leaders.

9:00 A.M.	Games and practice.
11:00 A.M.	Swimming.
12:00 Noon	Lunch.
1:00 P.M.	Talk by Leader
2:00 P.M.	Games, etc.
4:00 P.M.	Swimming.
6:00 P.M.	Dinner
7:00 P.M.	Evening Council
10:00 P.M.	Lights Out

IDEAS FOR EVENING CAMPFIRE PROGRAMS

- » Native Formal Opening
- » Braves to be sworn in
- » Choosing Names
- » First Aid
- » Fire-making
- » Caribou dance
- » Challenges
- » Water-boiling challenge
- » Closing

ONE-DAY HIKES

These are some rules I have found good in hiking: (Seton)

- » Do not go in new shoes.
- » Be sure your toe nails and corns are well pared before going.

» Do not take any little or weak fellows.

» Be prepared for rain.

» Take a pair of dry socks.

» Travel in single file in the woods and double file on roads.

» Take a Book of Woodscraft along.

» Always have a rule and tape line, knife, some string, and some matches.

» Take a compass, and sometimes a pocket level.

» Take a map, preferably the topographical survey.

» Take a notebook and a pencil.

» Do not waste time over things you can do as well, or better, at home.

» At last, and most important, it is wise to *set out with an objective.*

Here are some samples of the ideas I have found useful as objects for a short hike in winter: (Seton)

To determine that hard maple (or other timber) does not grow in such woods.

To prove that a certain road runs north and south.

To decide whether the valley is or is not higher than the one across the divide.

To prove that this or that hill is higher than such a one.

To look for evergreen fern.

To get wood for rubbing-sticks, or for a fire-bow.

To get horns for a Caribou dance.

If there is snow, to take, by the tracks, a census of a given woods, making full-size drawings of each track – that is, four tracks, one for each foot, and also give the distance to the next set.

If there is snow, to determine whether there are any skunk dens in the woods, by following every skunk trail until it brings you to its owner's home.

Now, be it remembered that, though I always set out with an object, I find it wise to change, whenever, after I get there, some much more alluring pursuit or opportunity turns up. Anyone who sticks to a plan, merely because he started that way, when it turns out to be far from the best, is not only unwise, he is stupid and obstinate.

ROPE WORK

The following are standard knots that an accomplished camper should know:

Square Knot	Floor Lashing
Two Half Hitches	Square Lashing
Taut-Line Hitch	Diagonal Lashing
Bowline	Shear Lashing
Sheet Bend	Tripod Lashing

Timber Hitch	Trestles
Clove Hitch	Round Lashing

Learning Tools:

www.cragcards.com

www.NetKnots.com

www.proknot.com

The EVERTHING KNOTS BOOK, Randy Penn

OLD WEATHER WISDOM

When the dew is on the grass,

Rain will never come to pass.

When the grass is dry at night,

Look for rain before the light.

When the grass is dry at morning light,

Look for rain before the night.

A deep, clear sky of fleckless blue,

Breeds storms within a day or two.

When the wind is in the east,

It's good for neither man nor beast.

When the wind is in the north,

The old folk should not venture forth,

When the wind is in the south,

It blows the bait in the fishes' mouth.

When the wind is in the west,

It is of all the winds the best.

Evening red and morning gray,

Sends the traveler on his way.

Evening gray and morning red,

Sends the traveler home to bed.

Red sky at morning, the shepherd takes warning;

Red sky at night is the shepherd's delight.

So, also, the tree-frog cries before rain.

Swallows flying low is a sign of rain and high, of clearing weather.

The rain follows the wind, and the heavy blast is just before the shower.

Learning Tools:

www.farmersalamanc.com

OUTDOOR PROVERBS

What weighs an ounce in the morning, weighs a pound at night.

A pint is a pound the whole world round.

Allah reckons not against a man's allotted time the days he spends in the chase.

If there's only one, it isn't a track, it's an accident.

Better safe than sorry.

No smoke without fire.

The Bluejay doesn't scream without reason.

The worm don't see nuffin' pretty 'bout de robin's song.

Ducks flying overhead in the woods are generally pointed for water.

If the turtles on a log are dry, they have been there half an hour or more, which means no one has been near to alarm them.

Cobwebs across a hole mean "nothing inside."

Whenever you are trying to be smart, you are going wrong. Smart Aleck always comes to grief.

You are safe and winning when you are trying to be kind.

BIRD HOUSES - BAT BOXES - BUTTERFLY HOUSES

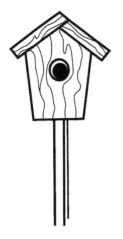 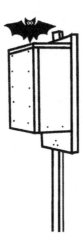 

Learning Tools:

"Making of a Hollow Tree" Ernest Thompson Seton

"Nesting Box's" National Wildlife Federation www.NWF.org

"How to make your own Bird Box" Gardeners World
www.gardenersworld.com

RUBBING-STICK FIRE

Rubbing-Stick Fire:

Obtain a piece of dry, sound, balsam-fir wood (or else cedar, cypress, Tamarac, basswood or cottonwood, in order of choice) and make of it a drill and a block.

Drill: Find five eights of an inch thick, twelve to fifteen inches long and roughly rounded, sharpened at each end.

Block, or Board: two inches wide, six to eight inches long, five eights of an inch thick. In this block, near one end, cut a side notch one half an inch deep, wider on the underside; and near its end half an inch from the edge make a little hollow or pit in the top of the block.

Tinder: For tinder, use a wad of fine, soft, very dry, dead grass mixed with shredded cedar bark, birch bark or even cedar wood scraped in to a soft mass.

Bow: Make a bow of any bent stick two feet long, with a strong buckskin or belt-lacing thong on it.

Socket: Finally, you need a socket. This simple little thing is made in many different ways. Sometimes I use a pine or hemlock knot with a pit one quarter inch deep, made by boring with the knife point. But it is a great help to have one made of a smooth, hard stone or marble, set in wood; the stone or marble having in it a smooth, round pit three eights inch wide and three eights inch deep. The one I use most was made by the Eskimo.

To make the fire:

Under the notch in the fire-block set a thin chip. Turn the leather thong of the bow once around the drill: the thong should be quite tight. Put one point of the drill into the pit of the block, and the upper end put the socket, which is held in the left hand, with the top of the drill in the hole of the stone. Always hold the left wrist against the left shin, and the left foot on the fire-block to hold all steady and in place.

Draw the right hand back and forth steadily on level and the full length of the bow. This causes the drill to twirl in the pit. Soon it bores in, grinding out powder, which soon begins to smoke. When there is a great volume of smoke from a growing pile of black powder you know that you have a spark. Cautiously lift the block, leaving the smoking powder on the chip. Fan this with your hand till the live coal appears. Now, put a wad of the tinder gently on the spark; raise the chip to a convenient height, and blow till it bursts into flame.

The notch much reach the middle of the fire-pit.

You must hold the *drill steadily* upright, and cannot do so without bracing the left wrist against the left shin, and having the block on a firm foundation.

You must begin lightly and slowly, pressing heavily *and sawing fast after there is smoke.*

If the fire does not come, it is because you have not followed these instructions.

STARS

The stars are the principle study for outdoors at night and above all in winter. Not only are many of the woodscraft pursuits impossible now, but the nights are long, the sky is clear, and some of the most famous constellations are visible to us only in winter.

So far as there is a central point in our heavens, that point is the North Star – Polaris. Around this all the stars in the sky seem to turn once in twenty-four hours. It is easily discovered by the help of the Dippers.

For example, if you do not know the Big Dipper, get someone who does to point it out or look in the northern sky for the shape of a Dipper, remembering that it goes around the North Star every twenty-four hours, so that at different times it is seen at different places.

Having found the Big Dipper, note carefully the two stars on the outer rim of the Dipper bowl are called Pointers, because they point to, or nearly to, the North Star; the latter being about three dipper rims away from the Dipper.

Now, we have found the great North Star, which is called by the First Peoples the "Star that never moves" and the Home Star." Note that it is in the end of the handle of the Little Dipper, or, as it is called, the Little Bear, *Ursa minor*

Now, let us take another view of the Big Dipper, *Ursa major*. Its handle is really the tail of the Great Bear. From the North Star, you will be able to identify other constellations. Can you find the Milky Way? Now, how many constellations have you learned? Make sure you are keeping a written record of your sightings.

PLANETS

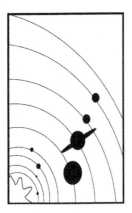

The stars we see are suns like our Sun, giving out light to worlds that go around them as our world goes around our Sun; as these worlds do not give light, and are a long way off, we cannot see them. But around our own Sun are several worlds besides ours. They are very near to us, and we can see them by the reflected light of the Sun. These are called "planets" or "wanderers." Because, before their courses were understood, they seemed to wander about, all over the sky, unlike the fixed stars.

They are so close to us that their distance and sizes are easily measured. They do not twinkle. There are eight, in all, not counting the small Planetoids like Pluto; but only those as large as stars of the first magnitude concern us. They are here in order of nearness to the Sun:

Mercury

The Planet with the second highest temperature in the Solar System and the closest planet to the Sun. Mercury is always closest to the Sun, so that it is usually lost in the glow of the twilight or of the vapors of the horizon, where it shows like a globule of quicksilver. It has phases and quarters like the Moon.

Venus

The warmest planet. The brightest of all the stars is Venus; far brighter than Sirius. It is the Morning Star, the Evening Star, the Shepherd's Star, and yet not ˘ star at all, but ˘ planet. It has phases and quarters like the Moon.

Earth

The only planet in the solar system that is known to have life. It has one natural satellite, the Moon.

Mars

Sometimes called the "red planet" and "the brother of Earth". Mars is the closest planet to the Earth. It has phases like the Moon.

Jupiter

The largest planet in the Solar System. A first magnitude Planet, with five moons.

Saturn

Sixth planet from the Sun. It has giant rings around it.

Uranus

Seventh planet from the Sun. It has 11 rings around it.

Neptune

The farthest planet from the Sun.

Pluto

A dwarf planet.

MOON

The Moon is one fifth the diameter of the Earth, about one fifth of the bulk, and is about a quarter million miles away. Its course, while very irregular, is nearly the same as the apparent course of the Sun. But in winter the full Moon is at an altitude in the sky near the limit attained by the Sun in summer. The Moon goes around the Earth every twenty-seven and a quarter days. It loses nearly three quarters of an hour each night.

LOST IN THE WOODS

If you should find yourself lost away from your friends or your camp, STOP. Sit and think of what you have with you to use as a signaling device. If you have packed correctly, you will have a whistle with you to blow at regular intervals. If you do not have a whistle, locate a branch one to two inches in diameter and as long as your arm. Use this to beat the side of a tree or rock or better a hollow log. As a last resort use your voice. Stay where you are! Your friends will have a much better opportunity to locate you quickly than if you keep wandering.

The worst thing you can do is to get frightened. The truly dangerous enemy is not the cold or the hunger, so much as the fear. It is fear that robs the wanderer of his judgement and of his limb power; it is fear that turns the passing experience into a final tragedy. Only keep cool and all will be well.

HOME-MADE COMPASS

If you happen to have a magnet, it is easy to make a compass. Rub a fine needle on the magnet then on the side of your nose. Then lay it gently on the surface of a cup full of water. The needle will float and point north.

* The cup must not be of metal.

NATIVE CLOCK, SHADOW CLOCK OR SUNDIAL

To make a Native shadow clock or sundial, prepare a smooth board about 15 inches across, with a circle divided by twenty-four rays into equal parts.

Place it on a level, solid post or stump in the open. At night set the dial so that the twelve o'clock line points exactly north, as determined by the Pole Star and nail it down. Then fix a stick or pointer with its upper edge on the center and set it exactly pointing to the Pole Star, that is the same angle as the latitude of the place, and fix it there immovably. It may be necessary to cut a notch in the board to permit a sight line. The hours eight at night to four next morning may as well be painted black. As a time piece, this shadow clock will be roughly correct. The Natives of course used merely the shadow of a tree, or the sun streak that fell on the lodge floor through the smoke opening.

BUILDING A BOAT

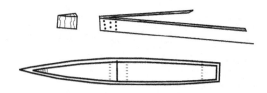

Winter is a good time to build a boat, if you have a workshop big enough to hold it.

The simplest kind of craft is the best to start with. Get two boards, smooth and with as few knots as possible, 15 inches wide, and 15 feet long If you cannot get a 15-inch board, use two or more narrow ones. Their joints can be made tight by calking. You will also need about 50 square feet of tongue and groove flooring, a piece of 2" X 6" scantling 15 inches long, and plenty of 3-inch nails.

Begin by beveling the stern post to an edge (a). Set this on the ground and nail two boards to it, one on each side (b).

At a point about 7 feet from the bow, put in a temporary cross piece 3 ½ feet Long (c), which can have the ends either plumb, or spreading wider toward the top.

Around this, bend the two side boards till their stern ends are but 3 feet apart. Nail on an end piece (d e) to hold them there.

Now cut a strip of 1" X 2" and nail it inside along the lower edge of the side board, so as to give a double thickness on which to nail the bottom.

Now, turn it over, remove the shaping board, put in the necessary stern and mid seats (see dotted lines), nail on a piece of board to double thickness where the oarlocks are needed – each about 12 inches aft the mid seat, add oarlocks, and the carpenter work is done.

Tar all the seams, caulking any that are gaping, and when the tar has set, paint her inside and out. As soon as this is dry, she is ready for the water.

She may leak a little at first, but the swelling of the wood has a tendency to close the seams.

This is the simplest form of boat. Great improvement can be made by making the sides deeper, and cutting the lower edge so that the bottom rises at bow and stern, also by setting the stem or bow-post at an angle, and finally by adding a keel.

Boat plans can be found at these websites:

http://www.spirainternational.com

http://www.hartley-boats.com

SIGN LANGUAGE

Do YOU know Sign Language? If not, do you realize that Sign Language is an established mode of communication in all parts of the world without regard to native speech?

Do you know that it is so refined and complete that sermons and lectures are given in it every day, to those who cannot hear?

Do you know that it is as old as the hills and is largely used in all public schools? And yet when I ask boys this question, "Do you use Sign Language?" they nearly always say "No".

The first question of most people is "What is it?" It is a simple method of asking questions and giving answers, that is "talking", by means of the hands. It is used by all Native Tribes, and by thousands of settlers today, in cities, as well as in the western country, and to an extent that surprises all when first they come to think of it.

Not long ago I asked a boy whether the policemen on the crowded streets used Sign Language. He said, "No!" at least he did not know if they did.

I replied, "When the officer on Fifth Avenue wishes to *stop* all vehicles, what does he do?"

"He raises his hand, flat with palm forward," was the reply.

"Yes, and when he means 'come on,' what does he do?"

"He beckons this way."

"And how does he say 'go left, go right, go back, come, hurry up, you get out?'" Each of these signs I found was well known to the boy.

One very shy little miss – so shy that she dared not speak – furnished a good illustration of this:

"Do you use the Sign Language in your school?" I asked.

She shook her head.

"Do you learn any language but English?"

She nodded.

"What is the use of learning any other than English?"

She raised her right shoulder in the faintest possible shrug.

"Now," was my reply, "don't you see you have already given me three signs of the Sign Language, which you said you did not use?

After collecting popular signs for several years, I found that I had about one hundred and fifty that are established. Yes. The sign for "yes" is so natural that one can see it instinctively made if we offer food to a hungry baby. That is simply a nod. No. This also is a natural sign. The sign for "No," when near, is shake the head.

Here are some of the better-known signs:

» *You* (pointing at the person);

» *Me* (pointing at one's self);

» *Yes* (nod);

» *No* (head shake);

» *Go* (move hand forward, palm first);

» *Come* (draw hand toward one's self, palm in);

» *Hurry* (same, but the hand quickly and energetically moved sever times);

» *Stop* (one hand raised, flat; palm forward);

» *Good-bye* (hand high, palm down, fingers wagged all together);

» *Up* (forefinger pointed and moved);

» *Down* (ditto downward);

» *Silence or hush* (forefinger across lips);

» *Listen* (flat hand behind ear);

» *Friendship* (hands clasped);

- » *Threatening* (fist shaken at person);
- » *Warning* (forefinger gently shaken at a slight angle toward person);
- » *Shame on you* (right forefinger drawn across left toward person several times);
- » *Scorn* (turning away and throwing an imaginary handful of sand toward person);
- » *Insolent defiance* (thumb to nose tip, fingers fully spread);
- » *Surrender* (both hands raised high and flat to show no weapons);
- » *Crazy* (with forefinger make a little circle on forehead then point to person);
- » *Look there* (pointing);
- » *Applause* (silently make as though clapping hands);
- » *Victory* (one hand held high above head as though waving hat);
- » *Indifference* (a shoulder shrug);
- » *Ignorance* (a shrug and a headshake combined);
- » *Pay* (hand held out half open, forefinger and thumb rubbed together);
- » *Poverty* (both hands turned flat forward near trouser pockets);
- » *Bribe* (hand held hollow up behind the back);
- » *Knife* (first and second fingers of right hand used as to whittle first finger of left);
- » *I am thinking it over* (forefinger on right brow and eyes raised);

- » *I forgot* (touch forehead with all right finger tips, then draw flat hand past eyes once and shake head);
- » *I send you a kiss* (kiss finger tips and move hand in graceful sweep toward person);
- » *The meal was good* (pat stomach);
- » *I beg of you* (flat hands tight together and upright);
- » *Upon my honor* (with forefingers make a cross over heart);
- » *Give me* (hold out open flat hand pulling it back a little to finish);
- » *I give you* (hold out open flat hand, but push forward to finish);
- » *Sit down* (drop flat hand sharply, palm down);
- » *Rub it out* (quickly shake flat hand from side to side, palm forward);
- » *Thank you* (a slight bow, smile and hand-salute, made by drawing flat hand few inches forward and downward palm up);
- » *Will you? Or, is it so?* (eyebrows raised and slight bow made);

If each of us would learn to use with precision the one hundred and fifty schoolboy signs and then add twice as many more, they would become fairly good sign-talkers. These additional signs they can find in the "Dictionary of the Sign Language."

Why should you talk in Sign Language? There are many reasons. In this *code*, you can talk to any other person without an outsider knowing or understanding. It makes conversation easy in places when you must not speak aloud, as in school, during music, or by the bedside of the sick. It is a means of far-signaling much quicker than semaphore or other *spelling* codes, for this gives one or more words in one sign.

So much for its advantages; what are its weaknesses? It is useless in the dark. It will not serve on the telephone. It can scarcely be written. In its pure form, it will not give new proper names.

Remember then you are to learn Sign Language because it is silent, far-reaching, and the one *universal language*. Since it deals fundamentally with ideas, we avoid words and letters, but for proper names it is very necessary to know the on-hand manual alphabet.

For numbers, we use the fingers, as probably did the earliest men who counted.

To learn more, go to:

www.lifeprint.com

www.handspeak.com

PICTURE WRITING

Brothers

Pictographs

The written form of Sign Language is the picture – writing also called Pictography, and Ideography, because it represents *ideas* and not words or letters. It is widely believed that Sign Language is the oldest of all languages and that indeed it existed among animals before man appeared on the earth. It is universally accepted that ideography is the oldest of all writing. To come a little nearer home, our alphabet is said to be descended from hieroglyphic ideographs.

We may also record our Sign Language in picture – writing, as was the custom of many Native Tribes, and we shall find it worthwhile for several reasons. It is the Native special writing. It is picturesque and useful for decoration and it can be read by any Native no matter what language he speaks. Indeed, I think it probable that a pictograph inscription dug up 10,000 years from now would be read, whether our language was understood or not.

In general, picture writing aims to give on paper the idea of the Sign Language without first turning it into sounds. In the dictionary of Sign Language, I give the written form after each of the signs that has a well-established or possible symbol. Many of these are drawn from Natives who were among the best scouts and above all noted for their use of the picture – writing. A few of them will serve to illustrate.

Numbers were originally fingers held up, and five was the whole hand, while ten was a double hand. We can see traces of this origin in the Roman style numeration.

A one-night camp, a more permanent camp, a village and a town are all shown in legible symbols.

An enemy, sometimes expresses as a "snake," recalls our own "snake in the grass." A "friend," was a man with a branch of a tree; because this was commonly used as a flag of truce and had indeed the same meaning as our olive branch. The "treaty" is easily read and was a pair of figures like this done in Wampum that recorded Penn's Treaty.

"Good" is sometimes given as a circle full of lines all straight and level, and for "bad" they are crooked and contrary. The wavy lines stood for water, so good water is clearly indicated. The three arrows massed mean that at three arrows flights in that direction, that is a quarter mile, there is good water. If there was but one arrow and it pointed straight down that meant "good water here," if it pointed down and outward it meant "Good water at a little distance." If the arrow was raised to carry far, it meant good "water a long way off there." This sign was of the greatest value in the dry country of the southwest. Most Native lodges were decorated with pictographs depicting in some cases the owner's adventures, at other times his prayers for good luck or happy dreams.

The old Native sign for peace, three angles all pointing one way that is "agreed," contrasts naturally with the "war" or "trouble" sign, in which they are going different ways or against each other.

An animal was represented by a crude sketch in which its chief character was shown, thus chipmunk was a small animal with long tail and strips. Bear was an outline bear, but grizzly bear, had the claws greatly exaggerated.

When the animal was killed, it was represented on its back with legs up.

Each chief, warrior and scout has a totem, a drawing of which stood for his name or for himself.

A person is represented by his totem. What will yours look like?

To learn more, go to:

http://www.whats-your-sign.com/native-american-symbols

http://www.symbols.com/native/

NATIVE TRAIL SIGNS

First among the trail signs that are used by Natives are still of use to the traveler. Among these some may vary greatly with locality, but there is one that I have found everywhere in use with scarcely any variation. That is the simple painted spot meaning, *"Here is the trail"*.

There are two ways of employing it - one when it appears on back and front of the tree trunk, so that the trail can be run both ways or the other when it appears on but one side of each tree, making a blind trail, which can be run one way only, the blind trail is often used by trappers and prospectors, who do not wish to follow their back track.

But there are treeless regions where the trail must be marked. Regions of sage brush and sand, regions of rock, stretches of stone, and level wastes of grass or sedge. Here other methods must be employed. A well-known Native device, in the brush, is to break a twig and leave it hanging. Among stones and rocks the recognized sign is one stone set on top of another and in places where there is nothing but the grass the custom is to twist a tussock into a knot. These signs also are used in the whole country from Maine to California.

In running a trail one naturally looks straight ahead for the next sign; if the trail turned abruptly without notice one might easily be set wrong, but custom has provided against this. The tree painted spot for turn "to the right" is the normal with an addition of a spot on the right side of the tree. Same with the left only opposite.

This is the Trail   Turn Left   Turn Right   Danger

To learn more, go to:

http://adventure.howstuffworks.com/destinations/trail-guides/understanding-hiking-trail-markers.htm

STONE SIGNS

These signs done into stone-talk would be as in the top line of the cut. These are much used in the Rockies where the trail goes over stony places or along stretches of slide-rock.

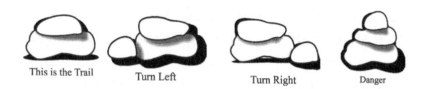

This is the Trail   Turn Left   Turn Right   Danger

GRASS AND TWIG SIGNS

In grass or sedge, the top of the tuft is made to show the direction to be followed. If it is a point of great importance three tufts are tied, their tops straight if the trail goes straight on, otherwise the tops are turned in the direction toward which the course turns.

The Ojibwas and other woodland tribes use twigs for a great many of these signs. The hanging broken twig like the simple blaze means "This is the trail." The twig clean broken off and laid on the ground across the line of march means, "Here break from your straight course and go in the line of the butt end," and when an especial *warning* is meant, the butt is pointed toward the one following the trail and is raised somewhat, in a forked twig. If the butt of the twig were raised and pointing to the left, it would mean "Look out, camp, or ourselves, or the enemy, or the game we have killed is out that way." With some, the elevation of the butt is made to show the distance of the object. If it is low the object is near, if raised very high the object is a long way off.

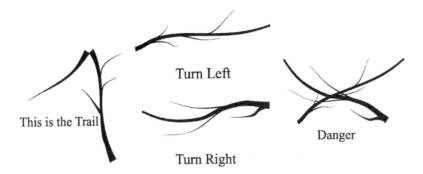

This is the Trail

Turn Left

Turn Right

Danger

SMOKE SIGNALS

There is in addition a useful kind of sign that has been mentioned already in these papers – that is, the Smoke Signal. These were used chiefly by the Plains tribes, but the Ojibway's seem to have employed them at times.

A clear hot fire was made, then covered with green stuff or rotten wood so that it sent up a solid column of black smoke. By spreading and lifting a blanket over this smudge the column could be cut into pieces long or short, and by a preconcerted code these could be made to convey tidings.

But the simplest of all smoke codes and the one of chief use to the Western traveler is this:

One steady smoke – "Here is camp."

Two steady smokes – "I am lost, come and help me."

I find two other smoke signals, namely:

Three smokes in a row – "Good news."

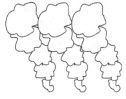

Good News

Four smokes in a row – "All are summoned to council."

All Come to Council

These latter I find not of general use, nor are they so likely to be of service as the first two given.

SIGNALS BY SHOTS

The old buffalo hunters had an established signal that is yet used by the mountain guides. It is as follows:

Two shots in rapid succession, an interval of five seconds by the watch, then one shot; this means, "Where are you?" The answer given at once and exactly the same means "Here I am; what do you want?" The reply to this may be one shot, which means, "All right; I only wanted to know where you were." But if the reply repeats the first it means, "I am in serious trouble; come fast as you can."

WEATHER SIGNALS

United States Weather Service Flags

Flags indicate at a glance what the weather forecast is for the area. These may change during the day and are generally updated at 10:00 am and 10:00 pm. Such flags can be found around ranger stations or parks, airports, beach communities, and other locations. The flags may be stacked for a complete forecast.

Also, how the flags are flying is a good indication of the wind speed.

1. solid white flag, clear or fair weather, no rain.

Fair Weather

2. solid blue flag, rain or snow.

Rain or Snow

3. black triangular flag, refers to temperature change. If it is on top, the temperature is rising. If on the bottom, the temperature is falling. The other flag may indicate fair weather or rain or snow.

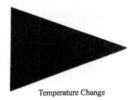

Temperature Change

4. white flag with black center is the cold wave flag

Cold Wave

5. White on top and blue on bottom means local rain or snow.

Local Rain or Snow

6. A red flag with a black center indicates that a tropical storm of sustained 35 mph winds.

Half Gale

7. 2 red flags with a black center means a hurricane or cyclone is coming with 75 mph sustained winds.

Full Gale

8. red triangular flag indicates information at the location.

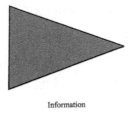

Information

Learn more at:

http://www.crwflags.com/fotw/flags/xf-weaus.html

CAMPING OUT

Every one of us looks forward to camping out, being in the outdoors, exploring, pushing ourselves to the limit and the adventure that comes along with it. Learning to become a self-sufficient person. Learning to build a fire, locate a camp, put up a tent, plan, cook, and enjoy primal outdoors living. Clean up after ourselves. The adventure of hands-on learning is the fun part.

Preparation is the key to a successful camp out. Learning and practicing the skills needed before venturing out is a must.

Look Out – Walk Out – Eat Out – Cook Out – Sleep Out

Camping teaches skills needed in the outdoors as well as at home and for life. It teaches through experience how to take care of yourself and get along with others in community. Be ready.

Begin with new Braves looking out a window and observing what is outside. Take a walk or a hike. Wear proper clothing and shoes for the weather and terrain. Pay attention to what you see and hear. Make sure each is keeping their journal.

Eat a meal outside you brought with you. Try to make it nourishing and filling. Try to bring what you need and not a lot of leftovers to deal with when finished. Pack out the trash.

Plan a simple outdoor meal that each has part in preparing, cooking or cleaning up. Fire building and safety are part of this step.

Now, if everyone has a bit of experience outdoors, plan an overnight camping trip. Enjoy the process and take each step in order as the Braves are ready to move forward.

10 OUTDOOR ESSENTIALS

This is a list of the **Ten Outdoor Essentials**. Those items each needs to have on hand to enjoy and be safe outdoors. A backpack is the logical place to store them. Check the condition and expiration dates regularly. Practice using maps, knives, and building fires.

1. Navigation
    »   Compass
    »   Map
    »   GPS
2. Emergency Whistle
    »   Cell or Satellite Phone.
3. Hydration
    »   Water Bottle
    »   Bladder
    »   Filter, Purifier, Chemical, Boil

4. Nutrition

   » GORP

   » Protein Bars

   » Emergency Rations

5. Rain Gear & Insulation

   » Rain suit

   » Poncho

   » Dry socks

   » Extra clothes / wool, polyester.

6. Firestarter

   » Waterproof matches & striker

   » Strike Stick (Flint & Steel)

   » Lighter

   » Fire tablets, candle, lighter pine

7. First Aid Kit

   » Size and amount determined on where and length of trip.

   » Cell or Satellite Phone.

8. Tools

   » Knife

   » Multi- purpose tool

   » Duct tape

9. Illumination

   » Headlamp

   » Flashlight

   » Extra batteries

10. Sun Protection
    » Sunglasses
    » Sunscreen
    » Hat
    » Emergency tarp
    » Space Blanket
    » Tube tent

PERSONAL GEAR

» Backpack
» Sleeping Bag, Pad, Ground Cloth
» Shelter, Tent, etc.
» Water Bottle, Canteen, Water Purification
» Mess Kit, Utensils
» Flashlight, Headlamp
» Pocket Knife, Multi-tool
» Fire Starter, Waterproof matches, Lighter
» Personal First Aid Kit
» Sun Protection, Hat
» Map & Compass

» Rain Gear

» Towel, Soap, Deodorant, Hair Brush/Comb, etc.

» Extra Clothing

» Food

» Insect repellent

» Mirror, Other signaling devices.

TENTS

There are many styles of small tents on the market. Choose one that will fit your style of camping. Make sure that it will fit the area of the country you will be camping in. A three-season tent will perform well in rain, wind, heat, and cold. Snow camping will require special equipment.

The First Peoples of the plains used teepees. They had a great advantage of ventilation and an open fire inside. It has the disadvantage of needing a lot of poles and of admitting some rain by the smoke-hole.

THE CAMP GROUND

Campfire

In selecting a good camp ground, the first thing is a dry, level place near good *wood* and good *water*. If you have horses or oxen, you must also have grass.

Almost all Native camps face the east, and when ideal, have some type of storm-break or shelter on the west and north. Then they get the morning sun and the afternoon shade in summer, and in winter avoid the coldest winds and drifting snows, which in most of the country east of the Rockies come from the north and west.

Sometimes local conditions make a different exposure desirable, but not often. For obvious reasons, it is well to be near one's boat-landing. Refer to Leave No-Trace Camping.

LATRINES AND SANITATION

Each small camp or group of tents in a large camp, must have a latrine - that is a sanitary ditch or hole. For a small camp or short use, this is a narrow trench a foot wide, surrounded by a screen of bushes or canvas. It is made narrow enough to straddle. Each time after use, a shovelful of dry earth is thrown in.

All camps should be left as clear of filth, scraps, papers, tins, bottles, etc., as though a human being had never been there. Have a plan for your garbage. Refer to Leave No-Trace Camping.

LONG TERM CAMP

As soon as all are on the ground, with their baggage, let the Leader allot the places of each band or clan. Try to have each and every dwelling-tent about 25 feet from the next, in a place dry and easy to drain in case of rain and so placed as to have sun in the morning and shade in the afternoon.

Each group is responsible for order up to the halfway line between them and the next group. Loose straw, tins, papers, glass, filth, etc., out of place are criminal disorder. Clear trash before setting up tents and leave the area better than you found it.

Pitch at a reasonable distance from the latrine, as well as from the water supply and garbage area. As much as possible, have each band by itself.

As soon as convenient, appoint fellows to dig and prepare a latrine or toilet, with screening. All will be busied settling down, so that usually there is no methodic work the first day.

But the second day it should begin. Be sure to acknowledge the difference between a weekend campout and a long term (generally 6 or more nights) camp.

CAMP OFFICERS AND GOVERNMENT

After the routine of rising, bathing, breakfast, etc., there should be called at eight o'clock or so a High Council. That is, a Council of all the Leaders, Old Guides or Medicine Men, and

Head Chief, that is, the Chief of the whole camp, appointed for that day. He is the Chief in charge, or Head Man of the village. It is his duty to appoint all other officers for the day, and to inspect the camp. In some camps this High Council meets at night when the younger members are asleep.

The other officers are:

Assistant Chief in Charge - goes about with the Chief and succeeds him the next day.

Keeper of the Milk and the Ice-box- when there is ice for the milk, etc.

Keeper of the letters - He takes all letters to the post and brings back all mail.

Keeper of the Canoes - No boats may be taken without his sanction, and he is responsible for the same.

Keeper of the Garbage - He must gather up and destroy all garbage each day at a given hour, preferably late afternoon.

Keeper of the Latrine - He must inspect hourly, and see that all keep the rules.

Keeper of the Campfire - He must have the wood cut and laid for the Council-fire at night, with an extra supply for all the evening, and must keep the Council-fire bright, not big, but never dull.

Also, the High Council should appoint a Tally Keeper for the whole camp. He is to serve throughout the whole period of the encampment, keeping the records for every day. Sometimes the work is divided, but one fellow can do it better, if he is willing.

A band or clan prize for the whole term is always offered. The competition for this is judged by points, and for each of the above services to the camp, the band, to which the scout belongs, gets up to 25 points per day, according to his efficiency.

No fellow should leave camp without permission. If he does so, he may cause his Band to lose points. Use a Buddy System – 2 campers who stay together during the whole camp. At times, it is better to have two sets of 2 buddies for safety in the wilderness so 2 can stay behind and 2 can go for help.

INSPECTION

Every day there is an inspection. It is best in the middle of the morning. The Chief and his second go from tent to tent. Each Clan is allowed 50 points for normal, then docked 1 to 10 points for each scrap of paper, tin, or rubbish left lying about; also for each disorderly feature or neglect of the rules of common sense, decency or hygiene, on their territory. That is, up to halfway between them and the next group. They may get additional points for extra work or inventions, or unusual services for the public good, but it is always as a Band that they receive the points, though it was the individual that worked for them.

After the inspection, the Chief announces the winning Band or Clan saying, "The Horns of the High Hikers were won today by _____ Band." And the horns are accordingly hung on their standard, pole or other place, for the day. At the end of camp, provided ten were present for at least a week, the Band that won them the most carries them home for their own and ever afterward is allowed to put them in one corner of their standard.

COUNCIL-FIRE CIRCLE

In every large permanent camp, establish a proper Council-fire Circle. The uses and benefits of these will be seen more and more, as camp goes on. This is the gathering place as appropriate and where the evening campfire is lit.

For the Council-fire Circle, select a sheltered, level place with a perfectly level circle. It should be prepared to accommodate the size of the group – 30 or 40 feet or more. At one side of the ring in a conspicuous place should be the Chief. In the exact middle of the ring is the Council-fire, never a bonfire. The fire should be bright, not just big. Leave room for dances, games, performances, skits, and songs.

Log Cabin

COUNCILS

Three kinds of Councils are held in the Council Place:

The *High Council* - with the Chiefs and the Old Guides every morning at 8 o'clock, and at other times when called.

The *General* or *Common Council* - the Council-Fire with all the fellows every night from seven to nine o'clock. At this we have some business (in the awarding of honors), some campfire stunts or challenges, and a little entertainment.

The *Grand Council* - this is usually held once a week during long term camps. Everyone comes in full regalia. Visitors are invited. Business except when very interesting is dispensed with, and a program of sports, competitions, and amusements, chiefly for the visitors, is carefully prepared. This is "Strangers' Night" and they should be entertained, not bored.

WATER

If there is a swamp or pond, but no pure water at hand, you can dig a Native well in a half an hour. This is simply a hole about 18 inches across and down about 6 inches below water level, a few paces from the pond. Bail it out quickly; let it fill again, bail it out a second time, and the third time it fills, it will be full of filtered water, clear of everything except matter actually dissolved.

It is now known that ordinary vegetable matter does not cause disease. All contamination is from animal refuse or excreta.

If there is no potable (tested drinking water) in the camp, bring it in with your supplies.

NOTE Always filter or treat any unknown source of water.

For more information:

www.Sawyer.com/products

MOSQUITOES, BLACK FLIES, ETC.

If you are camping in mosquito or fly season, the trip may be ruined if you are not fully prepared. For extreme cases, use the ready-made head-nets. They are hot, but effectual. You can easily get used to the net and no man can stand the flies.

NOTE Research which insect repellant works best for where you will be before you go. There are new resources regularly.

For more information:

www.Sawyer.com/products

SUGGESTED CAMP ROUTINE

6:30 A.M.	Turn out, bathe, etc.
7:00	Breakfast.
8:00	Air bedding in sun, if possible.
8:15	High Council of Leaders.
9:00	Scouting games and practice.
11:00	Swimming.

12:00 NOON	Lunch
1:00 P.M.	Talk by leader.
2:00	Games, activities, etc.
6:00	Supper.
7:00	Evening Council.
10:00	Lights out.

Sometimes High Council for a few minutes before lights out instead of in the morning.

CAMPFIRES

The day Columbus landed (probably) the natives remarked, "White man fool, make big fire, can't go near. We make little fire and sit happy."

We all know that a camp without a campfire would be no camp at all. Its chief charm would be absent.

Your first care, then is to provide for a small fire and prevent its spreading. In autumn, this may mean very elaborate clearing, or burning, or wetting of a space around the fire. In the winter, it means nothing.

You will use different kinds of campfires for different situations. Log-cabin, Lean-to, Tepee are the common designs. Prepare a fire the size you need for what you are cooking or to last a couple of hours for a council fire. Experience will help and also educate the need for more tinder than fuel.

You need:

Tinder - tiny pieces of wood, dead grass, dead leaves

Kindling – small sticks

Fuel – logs, tree limbs, branches

Campfire   Log Cabin   Tepee

COUNCIL FIRE

The Council fire is a very different thing from the cooking fire. There are just as many ways of making it wrong. Experience is the best teacher so mentoring is important for this skill. These are the essentials:

It must be easily started.

It must give a steady, bright light.

It must have as little heat as possible, therefore, it must be small.

A Log-Cabin fire is best built about two and one half feet high; the bottom stick about three feet long; the rest shorter and smaller.

The small wood and chips to light it can be put either under or on top of the second layer.

It should be drawn in toward the top, to burn without falling apart outward.

It must contain a large portion of dry, winter-seasoned wood, if it is to blaze brightly. The readiest seasoned wood is usually old lumber.

For an all-evening Council-fire, at least three times as much should be in stock as on the fire when started.

Log Cabin

NOTE A bonfire is always bad. It wastes good wood; is dangerous to the forest and the camp; is absolutely unsociable. A bonfire will spoil the best camp-circle ever got together. It should be forbidden everywhere.

GAMES AND STORIES

Some games from the original book:

CANOE TAG

Any number of canoes or boats may engage in this. A rubber cushion, a hot-water bag full of air, any rubber football, or a cotton bag with a lot of corks in it is needed. The game is to tag the other canoe by throwing this into it. The rules are as in ordinary cross-tag.

TREASURE HUNT

Players are sent out in pairs. A number of points are marked on the map at equal distances from camp, and the players draw straws to see where each goes. If one place is obviously hard, the scout is allowed a fair number of points as a handicap. All set out at the same time, go direct, and return as soon as possible.

Points are thus allowed:

Last back, *zero* for traveling.

The others count one for each minute they are ahead of the last.

Points up to 100 are allowed for their story on return.

Sometime we allow 10 points for each Turtle they have seen; 10 for each Owl seen and properly named; 5 for each Hawk, and 1 each for each for other wild birds; also 2 for a Cat; 1 for a Dog.

No information is given the Scout; he is told to go to such a point and do so and so, but is fined points if he hesitates or asks how or why, etc.

DUPLICATION

Take two boards about a foot square, divide each into twenty-five squares; get ten nuts and ten pebbles. Give to one player one board, five nuts, and five pebbles. He places these on the squares in any pattern he fancies, and when ready, the other player is allowed to see it for five seconds. Then it is covered up, and from the memory of what he saw the second player must reproduce the pattern on his board. He counts one point for each that was right, and takes off one for each that was wrong. They take turns..

This game is a wonderful developer of the power to see and memorize quickly.

SPOT THE RABBIT

Take two six-inch squares of stiff white pasteboard or whitened wood. On each of these draw an outline Rabbit, one an exact duplicate of the other. Make twenty round black wafers or spots, each half an inch across. Let one player stick a few of these on one Rabbit-board and set it up in full light. The other, beginning at 100 yards, draws near till he can see the spots well enough to reproduce the pattern on the other which he carries. If he can do it at 75 yards he has wonderful eyes. Down even to 70 (done 3 times out of 5) he counts Honor. 70 to 60 High Honor. Below that does not count at all.

FINDING TRUE NORTH

Each competitor is given a long, straight stick, in daytime, and told to lay it due north and south. In doing this he may guide himself by sun, moss, or anything he can find in nature – anything, indeed, except a compass.

The direction is checked by a good compass corrected for locality. The one who comes nearest wins. It is optional with the judges whether the use of a timepiece (like a sundial) is to be allowed.

TREE THE RACCOON

This is an indoor game, founded on the familiar "Hunt the Thimble." We use a little dummy raccoon either handmade or a ready-made toy. Sometimes even a little rag ball with a face painted on it.

All the players but one leave the room. That one places the raccoon anywhere in sight, high or low, but in plain sight. All come in and seek the racoon. The first to find it sits down silently, and scores 1. Each sits down, on seeing it, giving no clue to the others. The first to score 3 raccoons is winner, usually.

NAVAJO FEATHER DANCE

An eagle feather is hung on a horsehair, so as to stand upright, is worked by a hidden operator, so as to dance and caper. The dancer has to imitate all its motions. A marionette may be used. It is a great fun maker.

FEATHER FOOTBALL

This is an indoor or wet-weather game. The players hold a blanket on their knees or on the table. A soft feather is put in the middle. As many may play as can get near. They may in teams of 2, or 4, or each for himself. At the "Go!" each tries to blow the feather off the blanket at the enemy's side, and so count one for himself.

A game is usually best out of 7, 11, or 13.

ROOSTER FIGHTING

Make 2 sticks, each 2 feet long (broomsticks will do). Pad each of these on the end with a ball of rag. These are the spurs. Make an 8-foot ring. The two rivals are on their hunkers, each with a stick through behind his knees, his hands clasped in front of the knees, and the arms under the ends of the spurs.

Each tries to upset the other, to make him lose his spurs or to put him out of the ring, any of which ends that round, and scores 1 for the victor. If both fall, or lose a spur, or go out together, it is a draw. Battle is for 3, 5, 7, 11, or 13 rounds.

ONE - LEGGED CHICKEN FIGHT

In this the two contestants stand upon one leg, holding up the ankle grasped in one hand behind. Points are scored as above, but it is a defeat also to drop the raised leg.

STRONG HAND

The two contestants stand right toe by right toe, right hands clasped together, left feet braced. left hands free. At the word "Go!" each tries to unbalance the other; that is, make him lift or move one of his feet. A lift or a shift ends the round.

Battles are for best out of 3, 5, 7, or 11 rounds.

STEP ON THE RATTLER

This is an ancient game. A circle about three feet across is drawn on the ground. The players, holding hands, make a ring around this, and try to make one of the number step into the poison circle. He can evade it by side-stepping, by jumping over, or by dragging another fellow into it.

BUFFALO CHIPS

The players (about a dozen) put their hats upside down in a row near a house, fence, or log. A dead-line is drawn 10-feet from the hats and all must stand outside of that. The one who is "it" begins by throwing a small, bouncy, soft ball into one of the hats. If he misses the hat, a chip is put into his own, and he tries over. As soon as he drops the ball into a hat, the owner runs to get the ball and all the rest run away. The owner must not follow beyond the dead-line, but must throw the ball at someone. If he hits him, a chip goes in that person's hat and if not, a chip goes into his own.

As soon as someone has 5 chips he is the Buffalo and he loses.

WATCHING BY THE TRAIL

This is a game we often play in the train or on the ride to camp, to pass the time pleasantly. Sometimes one party takes the right side of the road with the windows there, and the other the left. Sometimes all players use all the windows.

The game is, whoever is first to see certain things agreed on and scores so many points wins. Thus:

	Points
A crow or a cow	1
A horse	2
A sheep	3
A goat	4
A cat	5
A hawk	6
An owl	7

The winner is one who first gets 25 or 50 points, as agreed. When afoot, one naturally takes other things for points, as certain trees, flowers, etc.

WATER BOILING CONTEST

Each is given a hatchet and knife, 1 match, a 2-quart pail, 7 inches or less in diameter, one quart of water and a block of soft wood about 2 feet long and 5 or 6 inches thick.

The water must be jumping and bubbling all *over the surface* or it is not boiling. If the first match goes out, contestants are usually allowed a second, but are penalized by having 2 minutes added to their time.

STORIES

GENESIS (OMAHA)

From the ritual of the Omaha Pebble Society

At the beginning all things were in the mind of Wakonda. All creatures, including man, were spirits. They moved about in space between the earth and the stars (the heavens). They were seeking a place where they could come into a bodily existence. They ascended to the sun, but the sun was not fitted for their abode. They moved on to the moon and found that it also was not good for their home. Then they descended to the earth. They saw it was covered with water. They floated through the air to the north, the east, the south, and the west, and found no dry land. They were sorely grieved.

Suddenly from the midst of the water up rose a great rock. It burst into flames and the waters floated into the air in clouds. Dry land appeared; the grasses and the trees grew. The hosts of spirits descended and became flesh and blood. They fed on the seeds of the grasses and the fruits of the trees, and the land vibrated with their expressions of joy and gratitude to Wakonda, the maker of all things.

THE QUICHE' CREATION STORY

This is the first word and the first speech

There were neither men nor brutes, neither birds, fish nor crabs, stick nor stone, valley nor mountain, stubble nor forest, nothing but the sky.

The face of the land was hidden; there was naught but the silent sea and the sky. There was nothing joined, nor any sound, nor thing that stirred; neither any to do evil, nor to rumble in the heavens, nor a walker on foot; only silent waters, only the pacified ocean, only it in its calm.

Nothing was, but stillness and rest and darkness and the night. Nothing but the Maker and Moulder, the Hurler, the Bird Serpent.

In the waters, in a limpid twilight, covered with green feathers, slept the mothers and the fathers. And over all passed Hurakan, the night-wind, the black rushing Raven, and cried with rumbling croak, "Earth!" and straightway the solid land was there.

ANIMAL STORY BOOKS FOR EVENINGS

A story is a nice way to end the meeting or the evening campfire. These are some old books to reference written by Ernest Thompson Seton:

Wild Animals I Have Known

Lobo, Rag and Vixen

The Trail of the Sandhill Stag

The Lives of the Hunted

Krag and Johnny Bear

Monarch, the Big Bear of Tallac

Animal Heroes

Biography of a Grizzly

Woodmyth and Fable

Biography of a Silver Fox

NATURE STUDY

BIRDS

Learn to identify your local birds. Observe birds from home, car windows, parks, at camp, and everywhere. Learn their names, both common and Latin. Listen to their calls, know where they nest, when they lay eggs, what they eat, and how to distinguish males, females and their young. Keep a journal of the location, time of day, and date you have located each.

Here are some links for other information:

www.Audubon.org

http://animals.nationalgeographic.com/animals/birds

Learn your local birds by sight and by sound. Here are some suggestions for your list. Keep a list in your journal of the location, time of day, and date you have located, seen, and heard each bird.

Bald Eagle (Haliaetos Leucocephalus)

Redtailed Hawk (Buteo Borealis)

The Barred Owl (Strix Varia)

Great Horned Owl (Bubo Virginianus)

Screech Owl (Otus Asio)

Turkey Vulture (Cathartes Aura)

Loon (Gavia Immer)

Common Seagull (Larus Argentatus)

Pelican (Pelecanus Erythrorhynchos)

Mallard (Anas Platyrhynchos)

Wood Duck (Aix Sponsa)

Trumpeter Swan (Olor Buccinator)

Whistling Swan (Olor Columbianus)

Bittern (Botaurus Lengtiginosus)

Great Blue Heron (Ardea Herodias)

Quale (Colinus Virginianus)

Ruffed Grouse (Bonasa Umbellus)

Dove (Zenaidura Macroura)

Flicker (Colaptes Auratus)

Ruby-throated Hummingbird (Trochilus colubris)

Kingbird (Tyrannus tyrannus)

Bluejay (Cyanocitta cristala)

Common Crow (Corvus brachyrhynchos).

Bobolink (Dolichonyx oryzivorus)

Baltimore Oriole (Icterus galbula)

Purple Crackle (Quiscalus quiscala)

Snowbird (Plectrophenax nivalis)

Song-Sparrow (Melospiza melodia)

Purple Martin (Progne subis)

Barn Swallow (Hirundro erythrogaster)

Mockingbird (Mimus polyglottos)

Catbird (Dumetella carolinensis)

House Wren (Troglodytes aedon)

Chickadee (Penthestes atricapillus)

Wood Thrush (Hylocichla mustelinus)

Robin (Planesticus migratorius)

Bluebird (Sialia sialis)

QUADRUPEDS

A Quadruped is any four-legged animal. Keep your list, with a description, a sketch, photograph, or casting of the track of local indigenous animals in your Tally Book. Look in your yard, park, fields, around camp, and anywhere you go.

Here are some links for other information:

www.naturetracking.com

www.enature.com

Some Common Quadrupeds:

Virginia Opossum (Didelphis virgiana)

Northern Flying Squirrel (Glaucomys sabrinus)

Southern Flying Squirrel (Glaucomys Volans)

Eastern Gray Squirrel (Sciurus carolinensis)

Least Chipmunk (Tamias minimus)

Black-tailed Prairie Dog (Cynomys ludovicianus)

Nine-banded Armadillo (Dasypus novemcinctus)

Striped Skunk (Mephitis mephitis)

Bobcat (Felis rufus)

Mountain Lion (Felis concolor)

Black Bear (Ursus americanus)

Eastern Cottontail (Sylvilagus floridanus)

House Mouse (Mus musculus)

Norway Rat (Rattus norvegicus)

Woodchuck (Marmota monax)

American Beaver (Castor Canadensis)

Common Raccoon (Procyon lotor)

Northern River Otter (Lontra Canadensis)

Coyote (Canis latrans)

Red Fox (Vulpes fulva)

American Bison (Bison bison)

White-tailed Deer (Odocoileus Virginianus)

American Alligator (Alligator mississippiensis)

SHELLS

Learn your local Shells by sight. A great time for shelling is right after a storm or at low tide. Here are some suggestions for your list. Keep a journal of the location, time of day, and date you have located each shell.

Here are some links for other information:

www.seashells.org

www.fws.gov

Fresh Water:

Elephantear (Elliptio crassidens)

Wasbash pigtoe (Fusconaia ebena)

Sheepnose (Plethobasus cyphyus)

Monkeyface (Quadrula metanevra)

Butterfly (Ellipsaria lineolate)

Salt Water:

Florida Auger (Terebra floridana)

Florida Cerith (Cerithium itratum)

Lightning Whelk (Busycon contrarium)

Turkey Wing (Arca zebra)

Jingles (Anomia simplex)

Banded Tulip (Fasciolaria hunteria)

Shark Eye (Polinices duplicatus)

Lettered Olive (Oliva sayana)

Beaded Periwinkle (Tectarius muricatus)

Pen Shell (Atrina)

Sunray Venus (Macrocallista nimbosa)

Angel Wings (Cyrotopleura costata)

Zigzag Scallop (Euvola ziczac)

Van Hyning's Cockle (Dinocardium vanhyningi)

Fighting Conch (Strombus alatus)

Coquina (Donax varibilis)

INSECTS

Insects are invertebrates and have six legs, two antennae and three distinct body parts. Learn your local Insects by sight and possibly by sound. Here are some suggestions for your list. Keep a journal of the location, time of day, and date you have located, seen, and possibly heard each insect.

Walking Stick (Phasmatidae)

Earwig (Dermatera)

Stonefly (Plecoptera)

Tree Cricket (Orthoptera)

Dragonfly (Odonata)

Mosquito (Diptera)

Stinkbug (Heteroptera)

Ant (Hymenoptera)

Scarab Beetle (Coleoptera)

Cabbage Butterfly (Lepidoptera)

Paper Wasp (Polistes Fucatus)

Horse Fly (Tabanus trimaculatus)

Mayfly (Ephemera Danica)

Firefly (Photinus)

Ladybug (Ladybug)

Here are some links for other information:

www.insectidentification.org

SPIDERS

Spiders are Arthropods that have two body parts, eight legs, and no antennae. Learn your local Spiders by sight and possibly by sound. Here are some suggestions for your list. Keep a journal of the location, time of day, and date you have located, seen, and possibly heard each spider.

Black Widow (Letrodectus mactans)

Brown Widow (Lactrodectus geometricus)

Brown Recluse (loxosceles reclusa)

Hobo Spider (Tegenaria agrestis)

Southern House (Kukulcania hibernalis)

Wolf (Lysoidae lycosa)

Huntsman (Heteropoda venatoria)

Garden Orb Weaver (Neoscona crucifera)

Daddy Long Legs (Pholcus phalangioides)

Tarantula (Aphonopelma)

Tick (Parasitiformes)

Here are some links for other information:

www.insectidentification.org

REPTILES

Reptiles are four limbed vertebrate animals that include Turtles, Crocodilians, Snakes, Amphibians, Lizards, and Tuatara of New Zealand. Learn your local Reptiles by sight and possibly by sound. Here are some suggestions for your list. Keep a journal of the location, time of day, and date you have located, seen, and possibly heard each reptile.

American Crocodile (Crocodylus acutus)

Loggerhead Sea Turtle (Caretta caretta)

Florida Box Turtle (Terrapene Carolina)

Red-eared Slider Turtle (Trachemys scripta)

Snapping Turtle (Chelydra scrpentina)

Gopher Tortoise (Gopherus Polyphemus)

Eastern Collard Lizard (Crotaphytus collaris)

Earless Lizard (Holbbrookia maculate)

Texas Horned Lizard (Phrynosoma comutum)

Carolina Anole (Anolis carolinensis)

Cuban Green Anole (Anolis procatus)

Texas Spiny Lizard (Sceloporus olivaceus)

Five-lined Skink (Plestiodon fasciatus)

Western Skink (Plestiodon skiltonianus)

Glass Lizard (Ophisaurus ventralis)

Gila Monster (Heloderma suspectum)

Rubber Boa (Charina bottae)

Here are some links for other information:

www.animals.nationalgeographic.com/animals/reptiles

AMPHIBIANS

Amphibians usually start as larvae, living in water. Undergo metamorphosis from larva with gills to air breathing adults with lungs. Learn your local Amphibians by sight and possibly by sound. Here are some suggestions for your list. Keep a journal of the location, time of day, and date you have located, seen, and possibly heard each amphibian. Up to 90% are frogs and toads.

Classes of Amphibians

Anura -Frogs & Toads

Caudata – Salamanders

Gymnophiona – Caecilians (none found in North America)

Here are some links for other information:

www.amphibiaweb.org

www.animals.nationalgeographic.com/animals/amphibians

SNAKES

NOTE All snakes are potentially hazardous. Do Not trap, capture, or handle any snake at any time. Observe from a safe distance. Keep a record in your wildlife journal of the date, time of sighting, location, and take a picture if you are able. Learn your local Snakes by sight and possibly by sound. Here are some suggestions for your list:

Poisonous:

Rattlesnake (Crotalus)10 North American varieties

Coral (Micruroides) 3 North American varieties

Copperhead (Agkistrodon)

Cottonmouth (Agkistrodon piscivorus)

Non-Poisonous:

Garter (Thamnopphis sirtlis)

Indigo (Drymarchon couperi)

Water (Nerodia sipedon)

Gopher (Pituophis catenifer)

King (Lampropeltis calligaster)

Pine (Pituophis melanoleucus)

Milk (Lampropeltis triangulum)

Rat (Pantherophis alleghaniensis)

Hognosed (Heterodon platirhinos)

Black Racer (Coluber constrictor)

Coachwhip (Masticophis flagellum)

Here are some links for other information:
www.discoverlife.org

FISH

Learn your local Fish by sight and possibly by sound. Here are some suggestions for your list. Keep a journal of the location, time of day, and date you have located, and take picture if possible.

Fresh Water:

Rainbow Trout (Oncorhynchus mykiss)

Largemouth Bass (Micropterus salmoides)

Perch (Percidae)

Catfish (Ictaluridae)

Black Crppie (Pomoxis nigromaculatus)

Chain Pickerel (Esox niger)

SripedBass (Morone saxatilis)

Salt Water:

Speckled Trout (Cynoscion nebulosus)

Black Gouper (Mycteroperca bonaci)

Sheepshead (Archosargus probatocephalus)

Red Snapper (Lutjanus campechanus)

Snook (Centropomus undecimalis)

Tarpon (Megalops atlanticus)

Bonnethead Shark (Sphyrna tiburo)

King Mackerel (Scomberomorus cavalla)

Permit (Trachinotus falcatus)

Here are some links for other information:

www.takemefishing.org

TREES

Take time to look up each of these trees. See which ones are in your area of the country. In the field, identify by leaf, bark, height, measure the girth, and keep a record of where the tree was located with GPS coordinates. Place this information into your outdoor journal.

White Pine (*Pinus Stribus*)

Red Pine (*Pinus resinosa*)

Long-Leaved Pine (*Pinus palustris*)

Tamarack (*Larix laricina*)

White Spruce (*Picea Canadensis*)

Hemlock (*Tsuga Canadensis*)

Balsam (*Abies balsamea*)

Bald Cypress (*Taxodium distichum*)

Black Willow (*Salix nigra*)

Quaking Asp (*Populus tremuloides*)

Balsam Popular (*Populus balsamifera*)

Cottonwood (*Populus deltoids*)

Black Walnut (*Juglans nigra*)

White Walnut (*Juglans cinereal*)

Pecan (*Hicoria Pecan*)

White Hickory (*Hicoria ovata*)

Big-Bud Hickory (*Hicoria alba*)

Pignut Hickory (*Hicoria glabra*)

Gray Birch (*Betula populifolia*)

Paper Birch (*Betula papyrifera*)

Yellow Birch (*Betula lutea*)

Ironwood (*Ostyra Virginiana*)

Blue Beech (*Carpinus caroliniana*)

White Oak (Quercus alba)

Yellow Oak (*Quercus Muhlenbergii*)

Red Oak (*Quercus rubra*)

Scarlet Oak (*Quercus coccinea*)

Black Oak (*Quercus velutina*)

Pin Oak (*Quercus palustris*)

Beech (*Fagus grandifolia*)

Chestnut (*Castanea dentata*)

White Elm (*Ulmus Americana*)

Red Elm (*Ulmus fulva*)

Osage Orange (*Toxylon pomiferum*)

Tulip Popular (*Liriodendron Tulipifera*)

Sassafras (*Sassafras sassafras*)

Sweet Gum (*Liquidambar Styraciflus*)

Sycamore (*Platanus occidentalis*)

Red-Bud (*Cercis Canadensis*)

Sugar Maple (*Acer saccharum*)

Silver Maple (*Acer saccharinum*)

Red Maple (*Acer rubrum*)

Box Elder (*Acer Negundo*)

Basswood (*Tilia Americana*)

Sour Gum (*Nyssa sylvatica*)

White Ash (*Fraxinus Americana*)

Black Ash (*Fraxinus nigra*)

Here are some links for other information:

www.arborday.org

NATIVE AMERICAN WAYS

SWEAT LODGE

A TURKISH BATH IN THE woods is an interesting idea. The Native Americans have always used this style of treatment and, with their old-time regard for absolute cleanliness, took the bath once a week, when circumstances permitted.

Their plan was to make a low, round-topped lodge, about five feet high and as much across, by bending over a number of long willow poles with both ends stuck in the ground. A few slender cross-bars lashed on here and there completed the skeleton dome. This was covered over with a number of blankets, or waterproof covers of skins, canvas, etc. A shallow pit was dug near one side. The patient stripped and went in. A fire was made previously close at hand, and in this a number of stones heated. When nearly red-hot, these were rolled in, under the cover of the Sweat Lodge, causing the intense heat, which could be modified at will. The more water on the stones the greater, of course, the steam. Meantime, the patient drinks plenty of water, and is soon in a profuse sweat. Half an hour of this is enough for most persons. They should then come out, have a partial rub-down, and plunge into cold water, or have it thrown over them. After this a thorough rub-down finishes, the patient should roll up in a blanket and lie down for an hour. Aromatic herbs or leaves are sometimes thrown on the stones to help the treatment.

This is fine to break up a cold or help a case of rheumatism. I have found it an admirable substitute for the Turkish bath.

The Native Silence

The first American mingled with his pride a singular humility. Spiritual arrogance was foreign to his nature and teaching. He never claimed that the power of articulate speech was proof of superiority over the dumb (non-speaking) creation; on the other hand, it is to him a perilous gift. He believes profoundly in silence - the sign of a perfect equilibrium. Silence is the absolute poise or balance of body, mind, and spirit. The man who preserves his selfhood, ever calm and unshaken by the storms of existence -not a leaf, as it were, astir on the tree; not a ripple upon the surface of shinning pool -this, in the mind of the unlettered sage, is the idea attitude, and conduct of life.

If you ask him, "What is silence?"

He will answer, "It is the Great Mystery! The holy silence is His voice!"

If you ask, "What are the fruits of silence?"

He will say, "They are self-control, true courage or endurance, patience, dignity, and reverence. Silence is the cornerstone of character."

"Guard your tongue in youth," said the old Chief Wabasha, "and in age you may mature a thought that will be of service to your people!"

CPSIA information can be obtained
at www.ICGtesting.com
Printed in the USA
BVOW06s1354311017
499050BV00049B/1241/P